The

NEW TREASURY

of

WAR POETRY

✳

The New
Treasury of
WAR POETRY

POEMS OF THE
Second World War

*

*Edited, with Introduction
and Notes, by*

GEORGE HERBERT CLARKE

Granger Index Reprint Series

BOOKS FOR LIBRARIES PRESS
FREEPORT, NEW YORK

INTERNATIONAL STANDARD BOOK NUMBER:
0-8369-6009-2

LIBRARY OF CONGRESS CATALOG CARD NUMBER:
68-58823

PRINTED IN THE UNITED STATES OF AMERICA

To Alexander Macphail

Soldier : Poet

O, how comely it is, and how reviving
To the spirits of just men long oppressed,
When God into the hands of their deliverer
Puts invincible might,
To quell the mighty of the earth, the oppressor,
The brute and boisterous force of violent men,
Hardy and industrious to support
Tyrannic power, but raging to pursue
The righteous, and all such as honour truth!

JOHN MILTON
Samson Agonistes

And not by eastern windows only,
When daylight comes, comes in the light,
In front, the sun climbs slow, how slowly,
But westward, look, the land is bright.

ARTHUR HUGH CLOUGH
Say Not the Struggle Nought Availeth

PREFACE

THIS ANTHOLOGY has been slowly built up since the outbreak of the war through the sifting of periodicals, the reading of lately published books of verse, and the co-operation of interested friends in Great Britain and North America. The Editor takes this opportunity of expressing his cordial thanks to all those who have made suggestions. Mr. E. C. Kyte, Librarian at Queen's University, and his able staff have kindly provided day-by-day facilities. Among these helpers Miss Melva Eagleson deserves special mention, since her diligent search often disclosed material that might otherwise have been overlooked. Dr. William Angus amiably shared the task of proofreading.

American and British preferences in the spelling of certain words have been respected by retaining American forms in the work of American poets and British forms in poems contributed from Great Britain or Canada.

Contents

✳

IV. FRANCE

V. RUSSIA

VI. CHINA

VII. NORWAY

VIII. CZECHOSLOVAKIA

CONTENTS

XIII. DUNKIRK

XIV. RAIDS AND RUINS

XV. KEEPING THE SEAS

XVI. THE FLYERS

XVII. THE FALLEN

XVIII. THE DICTATORS

XIX. THE CONQUERED

XX. INCIDENTS AND ASPECTS

XXI. REFLECTIONS

XXII. WOMEN AND THE WAR

XXIII. PEACE

ACKNOWLEDGMENTS

✻

THE EDITOR wishes to acknowledge the courtesies extended by the following authors, authors' representatives, periodicals, and publishers in granting their permission for the use of the poems indicated below, rights in which are in each case reserved by the owner of the copyright. Every effort has been made to obtain the necessary permissions, and any errors or omissions in listing them will be gladly corrected in future printings if called to the attention of the Editor.

Mr. L. Aaronson and *The Nineteenth Century and After:* — 'In the Time of the Persecution.'

Miss Mabel E. Allan and *The National Review of Literature:* — 'I Looked at England.'

Mrs. Phyllis Allfrey and *Harper's Magazine:* — 'Room Under Bombardment.'

Miss Elise Aylen and *Saturday Night:* — 'The Treason of Ganelon.'

Mr. Joseph Auslander and *This Week:* — 'Prayer to Jehanne of France.'

Mr. Leonard Bacon and *The Saturday Review of Literature:* — 'Easter Evening,' 'Our Time,' and 'Yankee Clipper.'

Mr. Peter Baker and The Favil Press, Limited: — 'Afterwards,' from *The Beggar's Lute.*

Mr. William Rose Benét and *The Saturday Review of Literature:* — 'Salute, Czechoslovakia!' and 'The Great Land.'

Mr. John Berryman: — 'The Moon and the Night and the Men'; '1 September, 1939.'

The late Laurence Binyon and Messrs. Macmillan and Company: — 'English Earth,' 'There is Still Splendour,' and 'The Voices of Hellas,' from *The North Star and Other Poems.*

Captain Earle Birney and The Ryerson Press: — 'On Going to the Wars,' from *David and Other Poems.*

Mr. Edmund Blunden and *The Times Literary Supplement:* — 'The Fine Nature.'

Mr. Victor Podoski, Colonel Antoni Boguslawski, and Messrs. George Allen and Unwin, Limited: — 'Dawn,' from *Mists Before the Dawn.*

Mr. Arthur S. Bourinot and The Ryerson Press: — 'Sleeping Now in Coventry,' from *What Far Kingdom.*

Miss Bianca Bradbury and *The New York Herald-Tribune:* — 'For the Quakers.'

Miss Audrey Alexandra Brown and *Saturday Night:* — 'Reported Missing,' 'The Phoenix,' and 'Withdrawal from Crete.'

Mr. Harry Brown and *The New Yorker:* — 'The Drill.'

Mr. Ivor Brown and *The Observer:* — 'Stratford upon Avon.'

Ann Watkins, Inc., literary agent for Mr. Roger Burlingame, and *The New York Times Magazine:* — ' "The Women Will Soon Knit Again." '

Miss Brooke Byrne and *The Saturday Review of Literature:* — 'Epitaph' and 'The Hosting.'

Mr. A. D. Peters, literary agent for Mr. Richard Church: — 'A House in War Time,' 'Something Private' (which appeared originally in *The Listener*) and 'Riding Up the Hill' (which appeared originally in *The Times Literary Supplement*).

Mr. Stuart Cloete and Messrs. Houghton Mifflin Company: — 'La Femme de Quarante Ans,' from *The Young Men and the Old.*

Professor Robert P. Tristram Coffin and *The Free World:* — 'At the Moon's Eclipse.'

Miss Mary Elizabeth Colman and The Ryerson Press: — 'The Cost,' from *For this Freedom Too.*

Miss Florence Converse and *The Atlantic Monthly:* — 'Descend, O Dante' and 'Liberté, Égalité, Fraternité.'

Mr. Robert W. Cumberland and *Queen's Quarterly:* — 'The Warden's Watch: 2 a.m.'

Miss Clemence Dane: — 'Trafalgar Day, 1940,' and 'Salute to Greece.'

Mr. Dudley G. Davies: — 'Migrants'; Mr. Davies and *The Empire Review:* — 'Vichy.'

Miss Babette Deutsch and *The Yale Review:* — 'Flight'; Miss Deutsch and *The Virginia Quarterly Review:* — 'To My Son'; Miss Deutsch and *The New Yorker:* — 'History.'

Mr. Patric Dickinson and *The Observer:* — 'Sailors,' 'War,' and 'World Without End.'

Mr. Sydney A. Sanders, literary agent for Lord Dunsany: — 'The Refugee' (which appeared originally in *The Fortnightly Review*).

Technical Sergeant Frederick Ebright and *The New Republic:* — 'Legacy.'

Lieutenant-Colonel Richard Elwes and Messrs. Hodder and Stoughton, Limited: — 'After Hearing the Prime Minister, April 27, 1941,' and 'In a British Cemetery Overseas, May, 1940,' from *First Poems*.

Dr. Ernest Fewster and The Ryerson Press: — 'Dawn,' from *Litany Before the Dawn of Fire*.

Mr. John Gould Fletcher and *The Saturday Review of Literature:* — 'The Attitude of Youth.'

Messrs. McKeogh and Boyd, Inc., literary agents for Miss Frances Frost: — 'Refugee in New England.'

Mr. Robert Frost, Messrs. Henry Holt and Company, and Jonathan Cape: — 'The Gift Outright,' from *The Witness Tree*.

Mr. Wilfrid Gibson and The Oxford University Press: — 'The Boy,' 'December Daybreak,' and 'The Sentry,' from *The Alert;* 'The Coast-Watch,' from *Challenge*.

Lord Gorell and *The Daily Telegraph:* — 'England, June, 1940,' and 'In the Fourth Year'; Lord Gorell and *English:* — 'Mother of God.'

Mr. Stephen Gwynn and Messrs. Constable and Company: — 'Stones of Greece' and 'We That Are Old,' from *Salute to Valour*.

Miss Amanda Benjamin Hall and *The Poetry Chap Book:* — 'For Madame Chiang Kai-Shek.'

Mr. John Hall: — 'Metropolis.'

Mr. G. Rostrevor Hamilton and *The Times* (London): — 'Atlantic'; Mr. Hamilton and *The Times Literary Supplement:* — 'Invocation.'

Mrs. Elizabeth Harrison: — 'Taking Off.'

Mrs. Agnes Aston Hill: — 'Recompense.'

Mr. Denis Hudson and *The Spectator:* — 'Valse des Fleurs.'

Mr. Emyr Humphreys and *The Spectator:* — 'Courage' and 'Cowardice.'

Mr. Rolfe Humphries and Messrs. Charles Scribner's Sons: — 'The War in the Dark,' from *Out of the Jewel.*

Mrs. Ada Jackson and Messrs. Cornish Brothers, Limited: — 'Widow-Mother,' from *World in Labour.*

Mr. Robinson Jeffers and Random House: — 'Two Christmas Cards,' from *Be Angry at the Sun.*

Mr. Lawrence Lee and *Queen's Quarterly:* — 'Fire-Bringers' and 'Take Up the Wings.'

Mrs. Mary Sinton Leitch and *The Richmond Ledger-Dispatch:* — 'Lidice'; Mrs. Leitch and The Alumnae Bulletin of Randolph-Macon Women's College: — 'Lines to a Dictator.' Both poems appear also in a brochure called *The Unseen Kingdom.*

Mr. Emmanuel Litvinoff and The Favil Press, Limited: — 'Not Revenge . . . But These,' from *Conscripts.*

Mr. F. L. Lucas and *The New Statesman and Nation:* — 'Dictator's Holiday'; Mr. Lucas and *Time and Tide:* — 'Spring-Song, 1939.'

'Lucio' and *The Manchester Guardian:* — 'Lidice.'

Mr. Archibald MacLeish: — 'Discovery of This Time.'

Sir Ian Malcolm of Poltalloch and *Blackwood's Magazine:* — 'Lament,' by Major George Malcolm, younger, of Poltalloch.

Mr. John Masefield, The Macmillan Company, and The Incorporated Society of Authors, Playwrights and Composers: — 'They Marched Over the Field of Waterloo' and 'To the Seamen,' from *The Nine Days Wonder.*

Messrs. Curtis Brown, Limited, literary agents for Miss Phyllis McGinley: — 'Dido in Tunisia' (which appeared originally in *The New Yorker*).

Mr. E. H. W. Meyerstein and *Queen's Quarterly:* — 'Two War Sonnets'; Mr. Meyerstein and *English:* — 'Phoenix': Mr. Meyerstein and *The Times* (London): — '*Domine, Dirige Nos.*'

Principal Nathaniel Micklem and *Queen's Quarterly:* — 'On the Frontier.'

Mr. J. E. Middleton and *Saturday Night:* — 'The Debt.'

Messrs. Brandt and Brandt, literary agents for Miss Edna St. Vincent Millay, and Messrs. Harper and Brothers: — 'Memory of England,' from *Make Bright the Arrows.*

Mr. Clark Mills and the Press of James A. Decker: — 'The Anonymous Lieutenant' and 'Valmondois,' from *A Suite for France;* Mr. Mils: — 'A Pastoral for Poland.'

Mr. Leo Minster and *The National Review:* — 'Warsaw, 27 September, 1939.'

Mr. Edwin Muir and *The Listener:* — 'The Trophy.'

Mr. Robert Nathan and *The New York Times Magazine:* — 'Captain Colin P. Kelly, Jr.'; Mr. Nathan and Alfred A. Knopf, Inc.: — 'Dunkirk'; Mr. Nathan and *The Saturday Review of Literature:* — 'To a Young Friend.'

Miss Muriel Newton and *English:* — 'Death in May.'

The New York Herald-Tribune: — 'High Flight,' by the late John G. Magee, Jr.

Mr. Norreys Jephson O'Conor and *Queen's Quarterly:* — 'The Viking Ship.'

Mr. Walter O'Hearn and *The Saturday Review of Literature:* — ' "For They are England." '

Miss Frances Taylor Patterson and *The Yale Review:* — 'Harbor View.'

Mr. Mervyn Peake and Messrs. Chatto and Windus: — 'London, 1941,' from *Shapes and Sounds.*

Dr. John Perrin and *English:* — 'Rejected Odyssey.'

Professor E. J. Pratt and *Queen's Quarterly:* — 'The Stoics'; Professor Pratt and *Saturday Night:* — 'Dunkirk.'

Mr. Frederic Prokosch, Messrs. Harper and Brothers, Messrs. Chatto and Windus, and the Musson Book Company: — 'The Campaign,' 'The Festival' and 'The Reapers' from *Death at Sea.*

The Proprietors of *Punch:* — 'A Soldier' and 'There is no Sanctuary for Brave Men,' by Miss A. G. Herbertson; 'Ivan' and 'Jan,' by Captain G. D. Martineau; 'Retreat,' by Virginia Graham; 'Trawlers,' by Hilton Brown.

Professor Oliffe Richmond and Messrs. Thomas Nelson and Sons, Limited: — 'Delphi,' 'The Moat' and 'They also Serve,' from *Song of Freedom and Other Verses in War-Time*.

Sir Charles G. D. Roberts and The Ryerson Press: — 'Canada Speaks of Britain.'

Mr. A. L. Rowse and *Harper's Magazine*: — 'Remembrance Sunday: Coombe Church, 1940.'

The Honourable V. Sackville-West and *The Observer*: — 'Personal Valour.'

'Sagittarius' and Jonathan Cape: — 'Good King Wenceslas Look'd Out,' from *Sagittarius Rhyming*.

Mr. Carl Sandburg and Messrs. Harcourt, Brace and Company, Inc.: — 'Take a Letter to Dmitri Shostakovitch.'

Miss May Sarton and Messrs. Houghton Mifflin Company: — 'From Men Who Died Deluded,' from *Inner Landscape*; Miss Sarton and *The Atlantic Monthly*: — 'Santos: New Mexico.'

Mr. Charles Schiff and *The Nineteenth Century and After*: — 'France' and 'Lidice.'

Dr. Duncan Campbell Scott: — 'Hymn for Those in the Air.'

Mr. Daniel Smythe, *The Saturday Review of Literature*, and Anderson House, Washington: — 'Transcontinental Bus,' from *Steep Acres*.

Miss Helen Spalding: — 'Curtain'; Miss Spalding and *The Spectator*: — '*E Tenebris*.'

Mr. Stephen Spender and *The New Statesman and Nation*: — 'To Poets and Airmen'; Mr. Spender: — 'The War God.'

Mr. Wallace Stevens and Alfred A. Knopf, Inc.: — 'Martial Cadenza,' from *Parts of a World*.

Mr. Arthur Stringer: — 'Taps at Twilight.'

Robert Thomas Hardy, Inc., literary agent for Miss Jan Struther: — 'Travelling America' (which appeared originally in *The Atlantic Monthly*).

Mrs. Rosamond Dargan Thomson and *The University Review*: — 'Panic.'

Mr. Lawrence Toynbee and *The Spectator*: — 'Castle Howard'; Mr. Toynbee: — 'November 11th, 1942.'

Miss Edith M. Tuttle and *The New York Times:* — 'Three Thousand Years After.'

Mr. Mark Van Doren and *New Directions:* — 'Crisis,' from *Our Lady Peace and Other War Poems.*

Lord Vansittart and *The National Review:* — 'Greece'; Lord Vansittart: — 'Moonlight.'

Miss Eleanor Wells and *The Atlantic Monthly:* — 'For the Undefeated.'

Mr. Laurence Whistler and Messrs. William Heinemann, Limited: — 'In Time of Suspense,' from the book bearing the same title.

Mr. T. H. White and *The Atlantic Monthly:* — 'Reading Giraldus Cambrensis.'

Mr. Oscar Williams and *The Nation:* — 'One Morning the World Woke Up.'

Mr. Andrew Young and *The Nineteenth Century and After:* — 'By a British Barrow.'

INTRODUCTION

*

WHAT is the business, the problem, the special concern of Poetry? Poets know, but the world, which finds poetry indispensable, has never too clearly known. No amiable conspiracy of poets and critics keeps the art alive. Because men and women desperately need its wisdom and its beauty, they have always guaranteed its existence. Since the creators of poetry are human beings and since all humanity is seized of imagination, singer and hearer mutually identify the ground-tone, the time-tone, as the bond that unites them. The bond is the poem, the poem the bond.

With what is Poetry concerned? The competing answers can be reduced to a single word — Life. Life itself is the continuing, never finished poem, an inexhaustible miracle of truth and trouble and delight, through its intense sensations, its crowding symbols, its tidal rhythms. 'The poet,' says Sidney, 'doth not only show the way, but giveth so sweet a prospect into the way, as will entice any man to enter into it.' Wordsworth finds Poetry 'the breath and finer spirit of all knowledge,' and Shelley praises it because 'it compels us to feel that which we perceive, and to imagine that which we know.'

Since Poetry is conterminous with Life, poetic diction cannot be mere prettification, nor poetic syntax an easy exemption from the discipline of style. More subtly and more searchingly than in any other of our human adventures, Poetry tries to reach and communicate pure truth. It is not much concerned with 'relative, comparative or temporal truths.' Its subject-matter is not a posted preserve bounding everyday reality, but consists rather in the thoughts of men's minds, the emotions of their souls, the thrust of their spirits.

War, thus, like faith and passion, change and hazard, wild

nature, mortality and immortality, has always been a theme for poets. It was a theme for Ezekiel; for Homer and Virgil; for the authors of *Beowulf* and *The Battle of Maldon*; for the metrical romancers and the balladists; for Spenser, Marlowe, Drayton, Beaumont and Fletcher, Shakespeare and Milton; for Blake, Cowper, Gray, Scott, Byron, Campbell, Tennyson, Browning and Walt Whitman. In our own time Hardy, Bridges and Masefield have explored it with marked insight and power.

War poetry, then, is not journalism, not official propaganda, not a mere footnote on an historical event or episode. Like all other poetry, it must come when it can and how it can — during the quick, wide vibration of the event, or within Wordsworth's formula of 'emotion recollected in tranquillity.' A true poem, whatever its subject — and its subject is always, in a sense, itself — results from an equation of both known and unknown quantities. There is always the plus *x*. It gestates, it becomes, it is — and we can say no more of it.

During the First World War many British and American poets produced stirring verses, some of them distinguished, many others still remembered. Among those concerned with the philosophy of war are John Freeman's *The Stars in their Courses*, Sir Ronald Ross's *Apocalypse* and *The Death of Peace*, and A. E.'s *Shadows and Lights*. Thomas Hardy's '*In Time of the Breaking of Nations*' (like Browning's *Love Among the Ruins*) presents a quietly effective contrast between war and love. Fourteen years afterwards Robert Bridges, in *The Testament of Beauty*, had stern, strong, valid words to say of war. Others, especially John Masefield in his *August, 1914* — perhaps the most *felt* poem of that war — have moved us by their understanding love of rankers and sailors who 'cannot be known.' Mr. Masefield's poem, written in heroic quatrains, has quiet sincerity, spiritual reserve, a deep sense of historical continuity, and a spare, grave beauty of style. Still others have written of particular incidents and aspects, of the peculiar genius of this or that region or country, of the bond of common suffering, of the wounded, of the fallen (the late Laurence Binyon's *For the Fallen* is the noblest of these laments), of the ministrations of women, of the battle-fleet, of the air-borne armadas, of merchantmen and mine-sweepers and humble fishing-boats, of the courage and tenacity of the fighting man, of the return of peace. Among the young soldier-poets of that war were Wilfred Owen, Charles Hamilton Sorley, Rupert Brooke, Robert Nichols, Wyndham Tennant, Robert Graves, Edmund Blunden, Siegfried Sassoon, the American Alan Seeger and the Canadian John McCrae. In this war, so far at least as Europe is concerned, everyone, because of raids and invasions (actual or possible) is in some sort militant, and many poets contributing to this volume, whether soldiers or not, have had occasion to pluck safety out of the nettle danger. In any case, as I have tried to show elsewhere,[1] the assumption that a poet on active service must reveal war more sensitively than his unenlisted fellow is hardly sound. The history of war poetry does not so attest. The poet's interpretation of war is a spiritual enterprise, conditioned upon his peculiar quality rather than upon this or that objective contact. Whether he wear khaki or not, he must *imagine* war. His first duty toward his art and his audience is to *be* a poet, to discover the timeless and placeless in the momentary and parochial, and to bring back a true and moving report of the experience of the human spirit during war's dark winter. Not infrequently, the muse of the poet militant — now as before — shows less interest in recollections of actual warfare and more in antidotal memories of home and friends and familiar scenes. Wordsworth includes this 'master-bias' in the picture of his happy warrior, and Lord Crewe, himself a poet, who lost a son during the Great War, has also touched upon this characteristic nostalgia.[2]

The tones and overtones of the war poetry of to-day are like and unlike those mentioned above. They are like, because the interval between the Peace of Versailles and the outbreak of the present war was itself, in all but name, a continuing world conflict, generating many of the same thoughts and themes; the

[1] *A Treasury of War Poetry:* Second Series (1919). Introduction, pp. xxx–xxxiv.

[2] Wordsworth: *Character of the Happy Warrior*, lines 57–64; The Marquess of Crewe: *War and English Poetry* (The English Association).

same longing for peace, freedom and security; the same division
between the forces of aggression and the nations that would use
their energies for nobler ends. In these respects the poetry of
the Second World War parallels that of the First, save for the
fact, as Mr. Michael Roberts has shown, that the renewed
struggle makes explicit what had long been implicit in the con-
dition of the world. Something greater than the present stage
of human worth and social justice is striving to be born. The
period of these two devastating wars may well prove to have
been its time of parturition. As a nobler world-order unfolds
we shall see more clearly, perhaps, the causes of these bitter
experiences and recognize them as evolutionary processes to-
wards a finer philosophy of life and purer modes of government
— individual, regional and world-wide. This war defines itself at
last as a battle in the endless conflict between power to do evil
and power to do good, which latter, as Bacon declares, 'is the
true and lawful end of all aspiring.'

In other ways, however, we hear new notes sounded in the
poetry of this great collision — tones that seem to be prompted,
first, by some sense of doubt and disillusion arising from the
unreal truce of twenty years; and, second, from the protesting
and innovating nature of modern poetry itself. Much of the
verse of the time, because its authors are gravely troubled and
baffled, has too self-consciously uttered itself in nervous obscu-
rities, strident satire, or street-corner gospels. Simplicity, sin-
cerity, the sense of eternality, recede and disappear. 'We ex-
press our age,' wrote Laurence Binyon, 'by resisting it, by
creating something which will outlast its fevers and its dis-
illusions.' [1]

Certain poets of our moment — by no means the most
thoughtful — insensitive to what Mr. T. S. Eliot calls 'the past-
ness of the past' and to its continuous presence, seem much less
companionable than their predecessors. May this not be due in
part to their failure to be friendly with themselves, to their lack
of self-integration as persons and poets, indeed to their want of

---

[1] *Tradition and Reaction in Modern Poetry.*

faith? The religion of the poet, on the intellectual side, must rest upon his belief in the worth of the universe during the long history of its evolution — past and future. On the side of feeling, he will be an active meliorist, even though, with Hardy, he would have us face frankly the worst that life can offer if we are to know our task and are really determined to reform our social and moral processes.

This anthology attempts a poetic survey of the objective deeds and experiences of the United Nations and of their subjective defences and advances as well. As we have seen, we are now in the third phase of a conflict that began in 1914 (or earlier), and since that date, even in the midst of war, uneasy truce and war again, the intellectual world has been sending forward its own patrols, consolidating its own front.

Not only in the section called 'Reflections,' but in many of the poems assigned to other sections, it is evident that our poets are exploring (even more carefully than they or their predecessors did during the first phase) the causes and the constitution of war, and that they are showing less reliance upon too simple expedients for outlawing it, less readiness to accept merely political and economic readjustments at the end. The great charters-to-be must come out of the thoughts and feelings of men who know what freedom means and what it costs — thoughts and feelings evoked by their poets and expounded by their philosophers. The fullest category in this collection records the thoughts of old men in their libraries, of young men in their camps, of all men who reflect even while they resist, endure, attack. Only free men can so reflect, and they know that this is the condition of their freedom. In William Blake's dramatic poem, *King Edward the Third*, the leader, invoking the spirit of Liberty, declares:

> The enemy fight in chains, invisible chains, but heavy;
> Their minds are fetter'd; then how can they be free?

It is hoped that the contributions to this volume will be found representative, in both form and spirit, of the poets' response to the condition of the world to-day. Well over a hundred poets, once, twice or oftener, strike here the various notes of challenge, hope, pity, irony, indignation, warning and prophecy. They have all seen visions that they must communicate, they are all in earnest, and — whatever differences their work may show in mood and music, fibre and skill — they have felt their themes. We must heed them, for they are ourselves made vocal. Many bear names long honored among us; of others, younger, we may be as yet less aware. Of none can it be said that he is but a 'school' sectarian. Although they cannot be one in personal opinion, imaginative power or range of influence, they remain one in spirit and intention, and the voices of the first and the least among them sustain their united voice.

G. H. C.

June, 1943

I. AMERICA

*

THE GREAT LAND

Things that are good and great my land has given,
of thought and word and deed, and heart and mind.
Now that the seas run high and night is blind
I will steer with mine own kind by the stars of heaven.
Yes, now that day goes dark and night glows red
and a wind is blowing as over desert sand,
my trust is with her living and her dead,
my faith bestead in the love of my own land.

Words that were harsh enough we have used against her
who nourished all our rage or gentlest thought,
who roused, who nobly urged, who subtly taught,
while with our small concerns we recompensed her. . . .
Now, with high thunderheads and the storm breaking,
by day, by night, she is song along my blood,
the great land we have seldom understood.
Behind my opened eyes the tears are aching. . . .

So I say, lift up your hearts where you see her striding
helmed and harnessed into furious dawn,
with her sons that crowd around her striding on
till all portentous evil find nowhere hiding;
and lift your voices too in a great shout
for victory's thunderclap on near occasions,
phalanx of eagles to free the captive nations,
stars in heaven no hurricane shall put out!

William Rose Benét

THE GIFT OUTRIGHT

The land was ours before we were the land's.
She was our land more than a hundred years
Before we were her people. She was ours
In Massachusetts, in Virginia,
But we were England's, still colonials,
Possessing what we still were unpossessed by,
Possessed by what we now no more possessed.
Something we were withholding made us weak
Until we found out that it was ourselves
We were withholding from our land of living,
And forthwith found salvation in surrender.
Such as we were we gave ourselves outright
(The deed of gift was many deeds of war)
To the land vaguely realizing westward,
But still unstoried, artless, unenhanced,
Such as she was, such as she would become.

Robert Frost

THE DRILL

I watch them on the drill field, the awkward and the grave,
The slow to action and the easily incensed,
The tall plowboys, the pale clerks, the fast men with a dollar,
The frightened adolescents, and those whose eyes explode
Like bombs or, like exhausted coals, lie dead.

They wheel and turn. The eternal convolutions
Of close-order drill — Right Flank or To the Rear —
Hold them as though, somnambulists, they moved

In the imposing caverns of some recurring dream
Where the only escape is to awake. But the night is very long.

The feet march on through the heavy summer morning.
The bodies are anonymous in their cotton khaki clothes,
And the faces, too, are all of a piece. Concealed at last from life
Are the weak chin, the nose too large, the forehead rutted and
          worn,
And the eyes too small, and the lips too fleshy or thin.

For the moment the accounts are all settled, the goods have all
          been sold,
The last delivery made, the last essay sent to the printer,
The elevator gone on its last strict voyage, the truck turned the
          last corner,
The last issue of bonds taken up, the last class attended,
The last row planted, the last payment made on the house.

The platoon moves past me on the field of summer,
The gray dust rising from the grassless ground,
Each man with his rifle resting on his shoulder,
Each man with his bayonet slapping his thigh, each man
With his eyes fixed on the man ahead, the corporals counting
          cadence.

The platoon moves past me into the mists of summer
And disappears into the darkness of our time,
A body of men, none known, none recognized,
Crossing my road for a little space. They go
Into the sun and the summer and the waiting war.

Seen for an instant and gone. Yet I felt between us
A bond not of country but of faith and love,
And I thought of an old phrase: 'Whither thou goest,

I will go.' And it seemed that the summer morning
Spoke out in a voice like song, that the air was full of singing.

And something said, 'They come and they go away,
The patient and the small. They go away into the sun,
Their names are forgotten and their few works also,
But when they go they take their weapons with them,
And they leave behind them houses heavy with honor.'

And I thought: It is enough. As I stood in a field
In Virginia in deep summer, while all around me
The trees dipped and the grass rustled, I heard the sound
Of platoons of men marching toward the crouching future,
And the voices of our approaching generations.

                                            Harry Brown

OUR TIME

Not in our time, America light-hearted,
Shall you smile at the sun,
Not in our time, for glory is departed,
That day is done.

Where is the spirit that is not convulsed
With bitterness of hate?
The burning blood that in the hot vein pulsed
Runs cold of late.

Toss off your cocktails at the Beach-Club bar!
Dive in the breaking wave!
Next year you will not do these things. They are
Not for the brave.

For brave we must be, past all heroism
That we as yet have dared,
Against 'raw horror and the blank Abysm
Of Death,' prepared.

But Death may give protection sacrosanct,
How ran the poet's cry?
'That no man lives forever.' God be thanked
That gangsters die.

But even if we see them underground,
We shall not make much mirth,
Having profoundly known the too profound
Grief of the Earth.

Yet in harsh times we must renew the gentle
And burnish bright the soul
With courage, vivid and unsentimental,
And self-control.

Count on true things, on wisdom and on loyalty,
From servitude of strife,
Win for our spirits liberty and royalty
Of Death and Life.

                                        Leonard Bacon

YANKEE CLIPPER

We're making sail on the Yankee Clipper.
Blow! Blow! Blow the Man down!
Though the gale that's rising is a white-eyed ripper
Blow! Blow! Blow the Man down!
It's a living gale, but we're making sail,
For we've sighted Moby Dick the whale,
Sighted him over the combers booming
On the far horizon fuming and spuming,
Seen his flukes on the skyline flailing,
And we'll make him sorry we took up whaling.
About we come, to the windward reaching,
Away to the place where we saw him breaching,
Heaving up from the deep profound.
And we're going to hit him before he can sound.
For we have conned and learned the part,
And we'll sock it to him with the bright long dart.
Nantucket, New Bedford! Be not afeared
Of such a whale as never was speared.
Deep though he sound, we know his path
And the iron shall smite him beyond Cape Wrath.
High through the breach, we'll do him under,
For all he may wallow and batter and thunder.
And we'll eat our chowder in New Bedford town.
Blow! Blow! Blow the Man down!

Leonard Bacon

*

II. ENGLAND AND AMERICA

*

TRAVELLING AMERICA

Travelling America, I am England-haunted.
   I seek new landscapes out of the window of the train,
But wherever I look, an England enlarged, transplanted,
   Springs to my sight, and carries me home again.

The clapboard house in a Massachusetts village
   Is a weatherboard house in Essex. From both, men sail
To plough their lives away in a dangerous tillage;
   In both, wives lie uneasy, an ear on the gale.

The Pennsylvania meadows are green and quiet
   As Penn's own meadows three thousand miles away;
The cattle browse, and the honeysuckles riot,
   And the streams run slow, and slow men cart the hay.

In Chesapeake Bay the woods come down to the water,
   Feathery-soft in the moonlight as funeral plumes:
I think of a small mother with a well-grown daughter,
   And remember the Devon coast and the wooded combes.

The Shenandoah Valley, the Blue Ridge lying
   Beyond it, the sound of crickets and whippoorwills —
This is the valley of Avon, with plovers crying,
   And daylight dying over the Malvern Hills.

Southward. Kentucky. Small fields, steep and stony;
   Patient eyes staring from a rickety shack.
(I've seen those eyes in Scotland, and the one cow bony,
   And the stunted crops, raised with a breaking back.)

Mobile. Biloxi. Rose-pink water-mallows
   Along the Gulf, in the marshes of Pontchartrain.

(The marshes of Kent are smaller; their creeks run shallow;
　　Their mallow-blooms are paler, and wet with rain.)

The grazing lands ... It is only the size that varies.
　　Mind's eye sees colour and shape, but has no scale:
It can gather the length and breadth of Nebraska's prairies
　　On the fells of Yorkshire, hard by Arkendale.

The orchards of Michigan and Minnesota
　　Are Hereford apple orchards in blossom-time;
And, climbing the long Black Hills of South Dakota,
　　It is still the Monadhliath that I climb.

But here, in the Southwest, opening my eyes on
　　Vermilion mesas rising from painted sands,
I have found at last a land with a new horizon,
　　A land which holds no echoes of other lands.

Here are cactus and thorn, with nightmare flowers;
　　Basalt and gypsum; trees long turned to stone.
Over the dried arroyo the red cliff towers:
　　Here is nothing familiar, nothing known.

Silence, and sun, and sand. The lizards flicker.
　　Ghostly and restless rolls the tumbleweed.
The eyes that gaze from the scattered huts of wicker
　　Are the secret eyes of an ancient and secret breed.

This is a country of dream, a world enchanted,
　　Improbable, fantastic, a wild release.
Here, and here alone, I can walk unhaunted.
　　I shall stay here long. Strangeness, at last, brings peace.

　　　　　　　　　　　　　　　　　Jan Struther

MEMORY OF ENGLAND [1]

I am glad, I think, my happy mother died
Before the German airplanes over the English countryside
Dropped bombs into the peaceful hamlets that we used to
      know —
Sturminster-Newton, and the road that used to run
Past bridge, past cows in meadow,
Warm in the sun,
Cool in the elm-tree's shadow,
To the thatched cottage roofs of Shillingstone;
Dropped bombs on Romsey Abbey where the ageing records
      show
(Or did a little while ago)
In faded ink and elegant fine hand
The name of a boy baby christened there
In 15— (I forget the year),
Later to sail away to this free land
And build in what is now named Massachusetts a new Romsey
      here.
(My ancestor, — I still can see the page,
Our sentimental journey, our quaint pilgrimage!)

Dorset and Hampshire were our home in England — the tall
      holly trees, the chestnuts that we found
Glossy within their shaggy burrs on the cold autumn ground
In the New Forest, new in the Norman's day, where we walked
      alone,
Easing at times our joyful weary backs
By shifting to a stump the weight of our small shoulder-packs,
Meeting no living creature all one lovely day
But trees and ferns and bracken and, directly in our way

[1]   printed by permission of the author and *The New York Times*.

Or grazing near at hand,
From time to time a herd of small wild ponies; well aware
Of imminent sunset and we two alone long miles from any-
    where.
All that we moved among — heath, bracken, hollies with round
    berries red
Bright for an English Christmas, beech and oak,
Chestnut, — with its sweet mealy food
On the leaves thick about us in the autumn air
Plentiful, gleaming from its rough burrs everywhere —
All this was good,
And all had speech, and spoke,
And all the magic unfamiliar land
Was ours by distant heritage and ours by deep love close at
    hand.

How many miles we walked I now forget, dog-tired at night
Spying an inn's warm light
Through small-paned windows thrown, —
To Romsey, and then back to Shillingstone.

So gravely threatened now
That lovely village under the Barrows' brow,
Where peering from my window at dawn under the shelving
    thatch
With cold bare feet and neck scratched by the straw
I saw the hounds go by:
So gravely threatened the kind people there,
She in her neat front flower plot,
He like as not
Up in the 'lotment hoeing,
Or coming home to his supper of beer and cheese,
Bread and shallots,
These thoughts . . .

And thoughts like these . . .
Make me content that she, not I,
Went first, went without knowing.

                    Edna St. Vincent Millay

*

III. ENGLAND

*

ENGLISH EARTH

As over English earth I gaze,
Bare down, deep lane, and coppice-crowned
Green hill, and distance lost in blue
Horizon of this homely ground,

A light that glows as from within
Seems glorifying leaf and grass
And every simple wayside flower
That knows not how to say Alas!

O Light, by which we live and move,
Shine through us now, one living whole
With dear earth! Arm us from within
For this last Battle of the Soul!

Laurence Binyon

1940

TRAFALGAR DAY, 1940[1]

They have dropped a bomb on St. Paul's —
'they,' for their name shall not live.
The roof was ripped up, masonry crashed
on to the table laid
before the inviolate Son.
Between the enormous walls
the Judgment infernal lashed
racketing round the nave,
till waves of thunder and dust
broke against Nelson's tomb.

[1] Copyright, 1940, 1941, by Winifred Ashton. Reprinted by permission
the author.

Even then, 'they' were not afraid.
They were proud of all they had done.
Nobody warned them, they did not know, none said:
'It is dangerous to wake the dead.'

For the Nelson spirit slips easily out of a shroud
into the morning, down Ludgate Hill,
slenderly moves in the crowd
hither and thither at will,
slipping between the people going to work,
stiff from a shelter bed.
Then somebody says: 'What flashed
like stars in a row, breast high?'
A girl says: 'A man passed by
with a pinned-up sleeve.'
A boy says: 'I didn't see.
I was watching the 'plane.' 'One of ours?'
'One of theirs, I believe;
but I heard a voice cry: "We
have characters to lose.
Those people have none." I say —
that was a voice! I could follow that voice.'
'So could I — and whatever order it chose
to give, I'd rejoice to obey;
I'd never once shirk.
D'you know what I thought it said?
"I'll not be satisfied with less
than twenty down."'
Yes! Yes! Yes!
Nobody warned them, they did not know, none said:
'It is dangerous to wake the dead.'

Then a wind drives along the Strand
till the dustbins rattle.

A gay, salt wind it is, with a rumour in it.
'I haven't the slightest doubt that a very few days,
almost a very few hours will put us in battle.'
'What's that?' they shout
from the taxi stand.
The same voice answers: 'Sooner the better, I said!
I don't like to have these things on my mind.'
Then the drivers turn in amaze
and stare.
On roves the whispering spirit,
leaving rumours behind.
'Things are beginning to happen at last,'
says London, bright-eyed.
'When we choose we move fast,'
says London pride.
'Tell us more!' But the spirit has passed
muttering: 'We must brace up!
The boldest measures are safest.... Let us attack!
Lose not an hour!... What? Leave off action?
I really don't see the signal. Nail mine to the mast!
That's how I answer such signals.'
There goes the frail little fellow, there,
turning into Trafalgar Square
just as the sirens blare!
From the pavement the pigeons rose
with a clatter and puff of wing.
They might have been guns, not close,
or 'planes manoeuvring.
'Caroo!' they gave their call,
'Caroo! We heard it said
often enough when we lodged with Paul
that it's dangerous to wake the dead.'

'Hear! Hear!' screamed the gulls
who ply between Channel and river.
'All the air is a-quiver
with the invisible news.
Nelson has stirred.
Nelson has left his bed.
Now let them shake in their shoes!'
Then, hissing with laughter, all the waves said:
'Yes, indeed we have heard
how dangerous it is to wake the dead.'

Then the waves tear after each other, pass and repass,
each agog to be first, breaking in spray,
welling and cresting the name they find easy to say:
'Nelson! Nelson awake! Tell the "Victory"!'
They tap at her side in the lulls,
they whisper: 'Nelson!' and flee,
racing after the ships of the open sea,
overtaking the Fleet,
tapping the news in code:
'Nelson — in London — awake!
He's in the ruined street.
He's in the byway and slum.
Nelson is everywhere.
He stands in the wreck of the road.
He sweeps up the broken glass.
He fights with fire and despair.
He feels for, he fingers your heart
till it beats in your breast like a drum.
This is the Nelson touch.
Pass on the news — he's awake!
Nelson expects so much.
Nelson expects that this day
each man, for the Island's sake,

will do his duty. Do they know in the North,
the South, the East, the West? Let it go forth —
news of our little man with the smile
and the four-fold star!
Carry to Copenhagen the tale of our Isle and our war!
Carry the news to the Nile,
to St. Vincent and Trafalgar!
"They" have waked Nelson, a spirit.
He slept sound in his bed.
And no one had warned them, "they" did not know, none said
how dangerous it is to wake our dead.'

Clemence Dane

October, 1940

BY A BRITISH BARROW

Let me lie down beside you, prince,
And share — no, do not wince —
Your grave for a short hour at noon
Shaped, with molehills for stars, like the full moon.

Man in this moon of turf and chalk,
If you can hear me talk
And understand a Saxon stranger,
Listen! to-day our country is in danger.

Does that not stir you, man of bones?
Your country it was once,
Yours when you strode across these downs
Where walls still wave about your hill-top towns.

Or is the news stale in your world
Where hosts are hourly hurled?

Perhaps you learnt from one of these
Who by his death gained a victorious peace.

You do not hear, man in this moon;
The skylarks might as soon
Hear me as you who are not there;
I waste breath that were precious now in prayer.

Andrew Young

'FOR THEY ARE ENGLAND'

For we are the people of England, who never have spoken yet —
Smile at us, pay us, pass us, but do not quite forget.
G. K. CHESTERTON

These are the last men
Who stand between us and a shapeless doom,
These are the little men who cannot die
Because they are so many millions strong.
These our defenders, stunted, gnarled and strong;
These are the life stream, having little but life
And giving what they have. They are the same
Who stood beneath another English sun
And fought Duke William's Knights. The bowmen they
Who swarmed at Crécy when the knights fell back,
Dealt chivalry its death blow with their staves.
These are the very men, the little men,
Eternal men-at-arms of England.

Last night dark shadows blotted out the sky,
Last night some heedless alien dropped from high,
Dropped on the Norman Church of St. Michel
His own dark blessing. Down the fragments fell

On a crusader's tomb. The noble lord
Gave little heed although his marble sword
Was broken and his visor grimed with dust.
He can endure it, as indeed he must.

But these are the last men, the enduring men,
These are the men who, gnomelike, from the mines,
Hard-handed from the fields, shop-worn, lathe-turned,
These are the men who ever and once again
Grumble and cheer and swear their common oaths
And stand their ground for God and England.

Like a dark stain across a picture book
Blotting the colours out, or like a brook
Defiled, across the England of the shires,
Hunt breakfast, cubbing, of cathedral spires,
Of Beecham concerts at the Albert Hall,
Pink book clubs and the Coronation Ball,
Of Ascot and the garrison Gymkhana
And all that pleasant other-world Nirvana
Falls the dark shadow of the new misrule.
The pleasant pageantry of church and school,
Varnishing Day at the academy,
Boats on the river, pomp and bended knee,
And Coward openings, artistic schisms,
The bright young people flirting with new isms, —
These all have had their day, nor was it right
That darkness should fall on it like a blight.
But he who knocks at freedom will not wait,
So pageantry must arm and risk its fate.

But these are the last men, the little men;
These are the men who yesterdays ago
Stood and watched cup-ties, bet in football pools,

Played darts and studied racing forms, the men
With tripes beneath their belts, oniony breath,
The common little men of fish and chips
To whom the cinema was luxury,
Men from the smoke-filled, sooty little towns
Who stood in queues and grumbled at the table;
These are the men, the common little men,
Who bawled hymns to their Chapel Deity
(and who shall say He was not pleased with them?),
And here are poachers and here are drapers' clerks,
Wheelwrights and joiners and fishmongers' men,
Gamekeepers, navvies, hawkers, felons even,
Men of all trades and none, masters and men,
Soft-voiced and slow, and others sharp like blades,
But in their eyes the hope of England,
And on their brows the stamp of England,
And in their hearts the strength of England.
Let the invader reading it beware,
'Ware the slow anger of the Englishman,
And having roused it, risk it if he dare.

On Dunkerque's last day the young squire died,
We saw him as we went out with the tide.
And knights of a new order mount the skies,
Smite the invader, snatch from him the prize.
Down plummets he who last night out of hell
Dropped ruin on the Church of St. Michel
And now is buried a matter of yards away
From the crusader's long-forgotten clay.
The young knights ride on to their rendezvous,
'So much owed by so many to so few.'
No one can better these new champions hail,
For by their deeds all other words grow pale.

But our talk is of the little men, the last men,
Who in a last unlikely reckoning
Would on the shores and rooftops, in the streets
And in dark lanes defend their England.
For these are the bowmen who broke chivalry,
These are the men who sailed with Francis Drake,
They are the men who wear the star of Mons,
These are the men who, with no playing fields
Behind them, stood their ground at Waterloo.
They are the men who always, in the end,
After the muddle was done and the work begun,
After the talk was done and the show turned real,
Stood and saved England — and will save it now,
For they are England!

Walter O'Hearn

THE MOAT

The little moat that fronts our fortress-wall
   Broadens about our isle till it is lost
In the once huge Atlantic — shrunk so small,
   It seems an inlet friendly to be crossed.

This rift in earth beneath so narrow a span
   Of traversable sky, where no feet tread,
Last breathing-space, the last trench left to Man
   Between his ruin and freedom's fountain-head —

Seven leagues of water and thin air that hold
   The embattled hordes at bay beyond the gate
Are charged with currents mightier seventyfold
   Than all Hell's engines, all the fires of hate.

A stormy strait of shallows, but its tides
   Well from Atlantic deeps, with every gale
Go prayers of nations: here the world divides,
   And Life is weighed against Death's loaded scale.

Here is the drawbridge of the free, whereby
   The waifs of Time had passage without let,
Whence brave men sallied oft abroad to die
   Thwarting some tyrant, and must sally yet.

Drawn is the bridge. Let the portcullis down;
   To break the assault be every rampart manned:
Better our fortress in the Atlantic drown
   Than yield the moat. Stand, brothers, and withstand.

But, as the tides fill half a world at flood,
   When half's at ebb, and Heaven their spring controls,
The tide of Freedom surges in men's blood,
   A force beyond their measuring fills their souls,

Till half the human kin is Heavenward drawn —
   Soon to restore the compensating tide
To thirsting wastes. Then lighten to one dawn,
   Confederate shores not Ocean can divide!
                       Oliffe Richmond

May 24, 1941

I LOOKED AT ENGLAND

I looked at England from a little hill,
Sharp scent of bracken in the summer air;
I looked across the valley to the still

Far gleam of water, to the rare
And sun-reflecting glow of ripening corn.

I looked at England when the light was new,
The shadows sharply etched across the vale,
The willow-herb soft coloured in the dew,
The woodland dark and secret in the pale
Cool glimmering dawn.

I looked at England when the dusk was near,
Quiet streams, and hedgerows pale with meadowsweet;
High on my wooded hill I saw the clear
Small stars above the pointed firs, and at my feet
The thin roads stretching to the unknown world.

I thought of war, and England seemed more dear,
Sleeping and quiet below my starlit hill;
I knew that I would fight, strong, without fear,
To keep that creeping horror from this still
And dreaming earth.

This silent, silvered world should never know
The noise of war; must never shake and cower
To sounds of alien feet. That river still must flow,
Brown-flecked and deep, knowing no battle hour;
Broad, cool and shining in the quiet fields.

Mabel E. Allan

*

IV. FRANCE

*

LIBERTÉ, ÉGALITÉ, FRATERNITÉ

Let us not fear for the creative word.

Though madness spreads its wings of fantasy,
Soulless and shameless, over a France bespelled,
Over a France betrayed, and wooing defeat;
Though from the Halls of Justice and the playgrounds
And fair façades of Paris and the ancient
Provincial capitals, those leaping letters
Vanish, besmeared upon and chiseled out,
Let us not fear: they shall not cease to burn
Behind the brow, to beat against the lips,
The sealed lips; they shall not cease to haunt
The echo in the prisoned heart of France.

We call them words, these three great attributes
Of the Logos; words, this life-stuff of the Spirit
From the Beginning. — We have juggled with them,
Delivered them over to the rant and bombast
And sentimental cant of politics,
Complacently: — and now the fate of the world
Hangs on these three we comprehended not.

So we, that knew not what we did, go down
To Doom? Heads high, too stupid to repent?
So the Dictator, with his bloody sponge,
Wipes off the dishonored motto from the face
Of captive, fearful, and bewildered Earth?
And generations crawl from slavish wombs
To people England, France, America,
With senseless robots, to eternity?

Defeatists! — In the Beginning was the Word.
We could not spawn a robot, breed a puppet,

Bring forth a soulless engine, if we would.
Though we be forfeit, still within our blood
Whisper the deathless syllables of life.

Let us not fear for the Creative Word.

Florence Converse

VALMONDOIS

After the coffee and the cognac at the garden table
we climbed where the path led, into the shadow of old trees,
or prowled the walls of the château, where no one stirred
at night or noon, or visited the mill that stood apart
to listen as the water on the wheel
chattered and chuckled, diamond-shrill.

                                   One day
in the fields, as we fled over the fences, someone cried
C'est un millier de boeufs, and then another,
Moi je dirais une dizaine,
while these looked on with mild abstracted eyes.

This was the place of afternoon. This was the place
that slept in an immense expanse of time.
Behind the slow pursuit of snails,
behind the long blond hair unwinding like the Oise,
a thousand violets in the grass, both blue and white,
and strawberry blossoms and lilies of the valley
shone through a mist of early leaves, like stars.

This was the place the bombers in formation chose.

Clark Mills

THE ANONYMOUS LIEUTENANT

While star-shells fell in showers of constellations,
like flowers the snow tufted the splintered branches,
blinded the sight of watchers at their stations,
sifted and shone from barricades and trenches.

Deep under the snow the strong roots wandered
and clung to darkness, rich for the new year;
dull through the dull air, explosions thundered
and anti-aircraft spat with reptile-fear.

That was November, the dead month. A current
of snow swarmed the white plain, the levelled walls;
transformed the trees into a plunging torrent
of branches; drowned the curses and the calls.

That was November. Flowers of the season
lay scattered everywhere, fallen and torn;
immobile, from horizon to horizon,
they sprawled astonished, faceless, or forlorn.

While star-shells fell in showers above the wood
and like no Angelus the guns resounded,
in these flowers the indifferent soldier stood
singing, and sang like August noon unbounded.

Helen, Helen, Helen,
the falling snow, the falling shell have fallen;
now that the deep night stirs and gleams
the drifting snow upon my shoulder seems
in the charged air
the touch of hands, or softer touch of hair.

Helen, Helen,
with rage I have been sour, I have been sullen
    and cursed the night and the dull hour;
forgot your hair, the enormous burning flower,
                and in your voice,
lips, breath, breast, limbs, no longer could rejoice;

                but now what I remember
is perfect as a leaf preserved in amber:
    how, under the high branches, sleep
flows like a tide between us, fathoms deep,
                till we awaken
and by the singing blood live and are shaken.

                Against the cries at night,
against the clotted snow, the stumbling flight,
    the sight of those on swollen knees
whose haven lies behind low stones and trees,
                against paralysis,
Helen, I conjure you and cling to this.

                Helen, Helen, Helen,
the falling snow, the falling shell have fallen;
    now that the deep night stirs and gleams —

And fell, as many of his comrades fell
who blown to pieces or outstretched on wire
were lucky; the survivors ran pell-mell,
coughing and crying under the cross-fire,

sobbing with haste, pursuing and pursued,
blinded by snow, fatigue, and rumored glory,
drenching an unmarked hill with sweat and blood,
whose lives create no myth, move through no story.

                                Clark Mills

PRAYER TO JEHANNE OF FRANCE [1]

O Jehanne, with the trumpets in your name,
By all the lilies of the Oriflamme,
By all the faggots and the final shame,
By all the burning voices at the Tree,
By all the visions that we cannot see,
By all you were that we can never be,
By all the little lambs, by every lark
That spilled a fiery fountain, spark on spark,
Of music to your heart, Jehanne of Arc,
By all your simple strength, and by the few
Straight words like light, and by the dream that grew
In your gray well-spaced eyes until you knew
The work you had to do —
The glory that flared up, and darkened, and withdrew,
The death they did to you —

Is this your France that made the great horn blow
Across the blood-red gap at Roncevaux?
Are these the mighty men
Who time and time again
Rebuffed the Roman, broke the Saracen?
Is this indeed the Gaul
Who stood, a terrible and living wall
Of flesh and blood and bone and spirit's pith compounded,
Forged in the furnaces of hell,
A solid mass
Chanting with hoarse monotonous iteration
The battle cry of a beleaguered nation,
'They shall not pass!'
(Christ, how that cry resounded!)

And drove the guttural and gloating Hun
Back from the very citadel
Of desperate Verdun,
Depleted and defeated and confounded?

O flash again, bright shield and furious lance,
And save the soul of France!
Strike down the traitor, cut the coward down,
The wolf and buzzard running beak to fang
In field and town!
Ring out, as yesterday you rang,
Clarion of hope, bugle of liberation,
To a bewildered and heroic nation
By knave and lout
Sold out,
The furtive coin clenched in the shameful fist
Of dupe and parricide and terrorist!

Ah France, beloved, brave and beautiful land,
On every side they stand,
On every hand
The dear magnificent dead,
A ghostly glorious band —
Roland and Oliver and Charlemagne,
And the tall Paladins who fought and bled
And with the uncounted slain
Fattened the kites of Spain;
And that bright-bearded captain-king whose name
Is a shooting star,
A flying flame —
Navarre!
And she,
The gallant martyr-maid of Domremy,
Who, when the hearts of men grew faint,

Rallied for Dauphin and for St. Denis,
Soldier and Saint,
The swords that set France free!

Ah sweet Jehanne, Jehanne,
Now that the spirits of your people languish,
And the grim traps are laid,
The sordid ambuscade
Wherein, convulsed with unendurable anguish,
France is once more betrayed,
Ah let your piercing clarion
Shatter this hideous trance,
This nightmare sickness in the soul of France!
Refuse this foul infection,
And, by the virtue of that proud rejection,
Rekindle, repossess
The sacred fire, the ancient fearlessness!

France is one vast Bastille;
The people turning and twisting under a vicious heel:
Your France, whose blood-soaked pikestaff banners gave
New hope to the oppressed, the prisoner, the slave;
Your France, that raised the heart like Lazarus from the grave,
Bends now her neck in the vile dust to kiss
A monstrous parody of peace.

Ride on, Jehanne, ride on and on and on
Through the thick darkness ringing your clarion!
Lightning of long deliverance,
Jehanne of France,
Jehanne! Jehanne! Jehanne!

Joseph Auslander

THE TREASON OF GANELON

The ageing king, the warrior,
Riding back from battle,
Riding with falsehood by his side,
Leaving the heights, the mountains,
Lifts his grey head and stirs uneasily,
Asking the false one:
'What sound is that?
Surely it is the horn of Roland
The unquelled horn of France
In battle still
That calls to us for aid.'
Answers the traitor,
Black-haired Ganelon:
'It is nothing.
Only the wind, only vain thunder
Echoing in the hills, in the narrow pass.
Let us ride on, my lord, in peace,
The fight is ended.
Let us go down through the fields
Where the folk are working,
Labouring for France restored.'
So Charlemagne rode on
With Ganelon.

The silent peasants working in the fields,
Reaping the corn that feeds their mortal foe,
Look up in wonder
Murmuring as they pass:
'Why rides not Roland with the king,
But only black-haired Ganelon?'
Fearfully they listen,

Asking in whispers
One to the other:
'What sound is that?
Surely it is the horn of Roland,
The unquelled horn of France
In battle still,
Calling the king to aid,
Like thunder in the mountains,
In the narrow pass;
Yet Charlemagne rides on
With Ganelon.'

There in the narrow pass,
Betrayed yet dauntless,
Roland, the heart of France
Still armed, still fighting,
Calls once again,
Sounds his last desperate blast,
Cries out in agony:
'France, oh, my king,
The fight is not yet lost
Though hardly pressed.
Why come my comrades not unto my aid?
Why rides my king, my France, with Ganelon
That he hears not my horn,
The unquelled horn of France
In battle still,
Calling for aid?'

In the Great Hall, the king,
The aged warrior,
Back from his battles,
Stirs as one in a dream,
Murmuring almost unheard:

'Surely it was the horn of Roland,
The unquelled horn of France
That called to me in vain
From the heights, the mountains.'
Hear the false lips that soothe him,
Black-haired Ganelon's:
'Oh, my dread lord, conqueror in many battles,
It was nothing, only the wind,
Only vain thunder echoing in the hills,
In the narrow pass;
The fight is ended.'

Elise Aylen

VICHY

These men lost heart and hope, let faith grow cold,
And sold themselves.   Small trafficking, thus far,
Were there not mingled with that dross a star,
The very soul of France; they would have sold
This with the rest, but it escaped their hold,
A shaken but still shining thing. There are
No treasons, no betrayals that can mar
Its radiance, it will kindle as of old.
Ancestral voices ringing over France,
Calais to Marseilles, Bordeaux to Lorraine,
Will cry: 'To arms, to arms! Our long mischance
Is done, the Gaul is on the march again.'
Then that false brood shall creep and crawl from sight,
Like jackals at the first return of light.

Dudley G. Davies

There was such yarn before, sheared from French sheep;
The Bourbons spun it, but they spun too much
And what was left was gathered in the dark
To make a fabric of the Rights of Man.
There was enough. And there was endless time.
Time has no meaning in a woman's mind
When she has ceased her mourning, closed her heart;
Only her hands move then, stitch after stitch.

On the steps, in the corners,
The women will soon knit again.
In the bistros, high behind the caisse;
Un Cinzano? Eh b'en, m'sieu, un schnapps?
Ça n'fait rien, I have not dropped the stitch,
This is for you, my boche, this little knot.
It is too weak? So, you will tear it, then,
As you have torn the baby from my milk?
Be tranquil, soldier, there are many years,
And many, many knots and endless yarn.
Here is another for égalité,
You would not know the meaning of the third.
Non, non, my boche, I knit to pass the time
And time is longer than the Soissons road.

Come, come, another schnapps, 'y en a beaucoup —
Non, non, my boche, I did not always knit.
I once made shells and once turned bolts for wings.
I once made flags and once I sewed the stripes
Upon a sergeant's sleeves, and even once
I made a man and left him by the road,
A little target for your splendid dive!
Non, non, monsieur, I did not always knit.
But I am knitting now to pass the time.
I know. It tires you to see my hands,

It gives you crise de nerfs to see them work
So fast upon my unproductive task.
You'll take it from me?   Call the Gestapo?
Be tranquil, then, my boche, for in your world,
In all your total world there are too few,
Too few police or soldiers or machines
To take our little knitting from our hands.

In the impasses, under the gas-jets,
On the worn steps, in the dim doorways,
In the forgotten culs-de-sac,
Behind the fish piles in the market stalls,
On the carrot wagons, up and down the Butte,
In the lost shadows of the Sacré Coeur,
In Notre Dame, behind the Madeleine,
The knitting women ply their yarn, click-click,
A row of stitches for égalité,
One for the Rights of Man in total peace,
And one for Brotherhood — the yarn is there;
We saw them shear the sheep to give us yarn
And there is time enough for Liberty.

Watch them, Hitler.
Watch them, Himmler.
Watch the knitting women.
Watch the women of France.
They have not lost their art.
The click of the needles is soft,
It will grow loud in the dawn of new communes.
You cannot tell it then from the spitting of fire,
You cannot tell it then from the bursts of the mitrailleuse!

                                        Roger Burlingame

*

V. RUSSIA

*

TAKE A LETTER TO DMITRI SHOSTAKOVITCH [1]

All over America last Sunday afternoon goes your Symphony No. 7, millions listening to your music portrait of Russia in blood and shadows.

You sit there in Moscow last summer a year ago writing music — and into the time of the falling leaves and the blowing snow writing music.

Sometimes as a fire warden you run to the streets and help put out a fire set by Nazi luftwaffe bombs — then you walk home and write more music.

When the Moscow radio tells the world what is news it reports the prime minister Stalin, Marshal Timoshenko — and the composer Shostakovitch.

On a long battle front sagging toward Moscow the Red army fights against the greatest war machine that ever marched into any country.

Dive bombers howl down like desperate steel hawks forbidden to ever sing any song unless it says death, death, death.

The flack, the ack-ack, the anti-aircraft guns send a rain of steel upward into the sky swifter than downward ever fell snow or rain in wild wind.

The tanks come roaring like elephants and land whales with hides of steel and a poison spit of lead meant to kill and kill.

[1] Reprinted by permission of Harcourt, Brace and Company, Inc.

Against these killers the Red army sets its traps and sends out its own tanks, artillery and anti-tank rifles meant to cut down Nazis and feed them death on death.

The outside world looks on and holds its breath and the American general Douglas MacArthur far over in Bataan radios Stalin: 'Magnificent! Matchless!'

And we hear about you, Dmitri Shostakovitch — we hear you sit there day after day doing a music that will tell the story.

These people, your people, named by the Nazi leader as 'bestial barbarians,' with no culture, no higher lights — your music is to speak for them?

So we see a people, near the awful trial of losing their capital city, telling the world they have a composer who writes music while the bombs fall.

In Berlin no new symphonies, in Paris, Brussels, Amsterdam, Copenhagen, Oslo, Prague, Warsaw, wherever the Nazis have mopped up and made new laws, no new symphonies.

And in Moscow you, Mr. Shostakovitch, 36 years old, having written six symphonies, go to work on No. 7.

The spring sun of 1942 melts the last of the snows and frost oozes out of the ground and the battle of Russia flares and cries again in the wrangling of steel and blood.

Summer comes and you Dmitri Shostakovitch see your music writing, your script, put on microfilm, a symphony held in a tomato can.

From Moscow across old Persia to still older Egypt, from Cairo round and roundabout to New York goes this little can of film.

Then what? Then the maestro Toscanini tells the NBC orchestra what to do with it and they put it on the air for the listening millions.

And how does it go and what do our ears make of it and what is it saying across the oceans and the convoys, the subs and planes?

Well, nothing like a fat man's race at a summer picnic, nothing like what a sugar daddy buys at a night club nor any certificate that guarantees comfort and convenience.

It begins calm with the good earth and with plains and valleys naked for the toil of man seeking crops and bread.

It goes on with touches like people in peace time having a chance to hunt for themselves their personal birds of happiness to listen to.

Then come drums and guns and evermore drums and guns and the war is on and the test of a nation and a people — and an ordeal for the whole family of man.

The music marches and fights, it struggles and kills, it stands up and says there are a thousand terrible deaths, it is better to die than to let the Nazis take over your homeland and tell you how you must live.

What you say sometimes Dmitri Shostakovitch is the same

as the message MacArthur sent by radio to Stalin: 'Magnifi-
cent! Matchless!'

The people of Russia may fall back and lose and lose and the
years go by and the time be long, yet in the end they will win.

They know when to be silent and suffer, when to fight and
how to sing while fighting, and how to say in the ashes and
blood loss: 'Neetchevo — it is nothing, what of it? It is for
our Russia!'

So some of us listened to what came in the tomato can from
Moscow to Cairo to Manhattan, we salute you and speak
thanks, Mr. Dmitri Shostakovitch.

Your song tells us of a great singing people beyond defeat or
conquest who across years to come shall pay their share and
contribution to the meanings of human freedom and discipline.

Carl Sandburg

IVAN [1]

Brave work, Ivan! Here's a New Year greeting!
  Rostov! Tikhvin! How those captures fall!
Rzhev! Kaluga! Evil rides retreating
  Back across the stricken plains he plotted to bethral . . .
    Brave work, Ivan!
    Comrade of the hidden heart!
Unexpected man of dreams who proved the best of all!

Old bold Ivan! Out in Death's own weather . . .
  Kharkov! Ilmen! How the names come back!

[1] Reproduced by permission of the Proprietors of *Punch*.

Borodino ... once again together!
  Cossacks plunging through the drifts along the tyrant's
      track ...
    Old bold Ivan!
  Friend we never learn to know!
Fire among the frozen mists that shone when all was black!

Tough stuff, Ivan! When the black tide scatters,
  Wings well broken, wheels worn down at last,
Long-tongued folk may talk of many matters:
  We shall know the name of him who stood and bore the
      blast ...
    Great grim Ivan!
  Breaker of dark dynasties!
Victor of his own wide fields that hold the storied past!

                       G. D. Martineau

*

VI. CHINA

*

FOR MADAME CHIANG KAI-SHEK

Madame — O Lady of the jeweled brain,
The steadfast, marching spirit and proud anger,
Whose mercies and whose justice can sustain,
Like tea and rice, a people doomed to hunger
Where dragon seed is sown — you that have toiled
To stanch a nation's bleeding and to patch
The broken hearts of men, their wives despoiled,
And death and dearth beneath the ruined thatch
That sheltered teeming life — embattled one,
Your dark head resting on an unsafe pillow,
I here salute you, moon to China's sun!

Your voice is like the breeze that stirs the willow,
Yet old as from the dynasty of Ming,
Your wisdom . . . Princess of the valorous ways,
Lest I affront you by this song I bring,
Forgive me the discourtesy of praise.

Amanda Benjamin Hall

*

VII. NORWAY

*

THE VIKING SHIP

Bygdö, Norway

Our boat thrusts steadily through the blue water;
Pulsing with life of engines, she leaves behind
The city surmounted by the flashing glass
Of modern buildings, edifices without eyebrows,
And glides to rest below tree-dotted streets
Which mark a town of country residences.

  Bordering this world of pleasant life and leisure
Stands the great building we have come to see,
Entrance to Nordic folk-antiquity.
After the brightness of the village street
The shaded whiteness of the plaster walls
Dazes with sudden coolness.   Time whirls away
As though a myriad clocks were racing backwards
And our bewildered minds annihilated
Space and distance.   Surrounded by an age
Of early history, we seem to hear
The sounds of progress faintly; tempest and fire,
The sea, the avalanche are immanent
With terror, overshadow us.   Above
Our heads black woodwork of a curving prow
Looms like a threatening crag until we see
The graceful lines of man-made symmetry.

  Huge, without motion yet ever moving forward,
The ship is like a leashed animal held
In check for centuries. From the broken mast
The sail rises in imagination; rowers
Again are bending to the oars, which waves

Almost tug from out their hands as lightly
The vessel sweeps from foaming crest to hollow
Dark with the shadow of the wave to come.
Fierce cries and clank of metal punctuate
The windy air; above them sound clear-voiced
The heartening phrases of the fair-haired queen
Who dominates her vassals.

                        Token of man's
Dependence on a might unseen, the serpent
Wrought from the toughness of the forest oak
In semblance of the Midgard Snake circling
The earth and swallowing his tail, rivets
Our gaze upon the towering bow
Slender and strong.

                    Touching, this ancient trust
In crude mythology, this giving form
To forces known and yet beyond control,
Perennial dread of final devastation.
The simple wonder of an earlier day
Lacks the stark horror of our modern dread;
The Midgard Serpent bears the trace of man's
Unconquerable imagination. To-day
The Snake of War is product of cold thought
And mechanized capacity; we sink
Beneath our cleverness, our age-long cry
To God, without avail from emptying churches,
And we at last about to be confounded.

                        Norreys Jephson O'Conor

*

VIII. CZECHOSLOVAKIA

*

SALUTE, CZECHOSLOVAKIA!

Verily the new day,
the New Order!
For the death of a butcher, for the bloody heel,
a village of poor folk, diggers in mines,
erased from earth, children torn from their mothers,
forcibly to be schooled in lies,
the fathers slain. Deliberate reprisal.
Murder added to murder added to . . .

Lidice, in its blood and agony,
forever living — in a newer day,
a newer order, otherwise than this . . .

'The name of the community extinguished'?
In fire the inextinguishable name!

Massacre of whole villages, the slain
in Belgium and the Netherlands, *five hundred;*
in France, *two thousand;* in decimated Poland,
one hundred and forty thousand; (Mark the score,
never forget the score!) in Yugoslavia,
three hundred and fifty thousand; gallant Greece,
over eight hundred and the people dying
starved and emaciated in the streets . . .

His fame was a murderer's fame,
Heydrich of the Gestapo,
Death's pander, and murder's — 'der Henker'
called Cobra for thin head, glittering eyes,
and deadly fang. Norway and Netherlands,
Belgium and France, knew him, knew the Hangman,

the Deathshead of Dachau — who lay in State
at the high Castle of the Kings of Prague,
Praha of old, on Hradčany the Hill,
an hundred towers, 'a fairytale in stone' . . .

A thousand years ago King Wenceslaus
(whom English children in the winter sing!)
founded the great cathedral — golden Prague,
'Rome of the North' — green of the summer fields,
white clustered houses, poppies in the barley,
hills of Moravia, the singing river . . .
The mountain-guarded land, like unto ours
in its great human dream — land of John Huss
and Gregor Mendel, and John of Nepomuk
whose lips were sealed upon a sacred trust,
he never would betray! Land of great forest,
of heat and cold and the Carpathian crags
where haunted castles moulder — of the singer
in the kraut market in the public square —
festival and costume, the Golden Lane,
the Alchemist's Street — Jews in their gabardines,
folk dress and factory shoes, the sturdy Sokols,
the laughing girls . . .

                         Where is that laughter now
since they who hold the bastion of all Europe,
they who were called 'the arsenal of the world,'
in that dark hour in which they were betrayed
lifted the bitter cup, who now endure
under the bloody boot, the cracking dog-whip,
under the hated swastika brassard
symbol of murder and plunder . . . under the new day
the New Order . . . that gives this happy land
a Reichs Protector . . . where the tortured scholar

and gentle spirit — jeered, obscenely reviled —
lies twisted in his blood under the windows sealed,
under the slogging footsteps of patrols
pounding the cobbles, the guttural bark of orders,
the fixity of Murder's frozen stare . . .

We mark the score. Silent, we mark the score . . .!
William Rose Benét

LIDICE [1]

All the buildings in the village have been razed to the ground
and the name of the village, Lidice, erased from official records
— German official account.

THE GERMAN SPEAKS:

This village has no name. We wiped it out,
   Blasted its streets and razed its dwellings low;
Its men we shot and drove a piteous rout
   Of little ones and women forth in woe.
Dead is the husband, gaoled the child and wife,
   Down are the walls and all the place is dumb;
We have erased it from the book of life,
   And none shall speak its name in years to come.

HISTORY SPEAKS:

This village has a name which shall for long
   Offer unyielding witness to a deed
Of savage infamy and hideous wrong,
   Born of a brutal and insensate creed.

[1] With acknowledgments to *The Manchester Guardian*.

For years that title shall tell on, untired,
   That here the German mood, the German shame,
Was seen in essence and in crime acquired
   An endless habitation and a name.

                       Lucio

LIDICE

Now let each common and heroic man
Be every stranger's heir and epitaph,
His testimony, and continuing kin.
Let him stand upright, and endure the rough
Assault and horror of a remote death;
Suffer the distant wounds, and drown afar.
Let him be torn, and buried. For, in truth,
Who is alive? Who, buried? All men are.

I am a Jew. Now every common man
Grows like to me; for I am grief. And yet
What common degradation has begun,
Common nobility may consummate:
The European dead crying out for rest,
I rest in them, and take them to my breast.
                    Charles Schiff

LIDICE

To the Despoilers

From what dark wine, with what disastrous gall
   Is mixed that brew where reason now is drowned,
   That thus malignant anger should be crowned

With folly? Bullets sing against a wall
Their song of hate and, making festival
  Of death, you trust that violated ground
  Will take and hold the guiltless in profound
And everlasting silence where they fall.

Silence? The wind shall bear on every gust
  Their voices over mountain, plain and sea!
In vain your shaking fingers shall be thrust
  Against your ears, however far you flee,
Till you implore the mercy of the dust
  As refuge from the name of Lidice!

Mary Sinton Leitch

*

IX. GREECE

*

THE VOICES OF HELLAS

Time, that has crumbled to impotent nothingness
Empire on empire, towering in arrogance,
Time, at whose finger invisibly commanding
Their bannered battalions marched to oblivion,

Time stays motionless when are heard the voices
Of Hellas, proclaiming over a wondering world
Wisdom and joy and the radiance of reality
Disclosed as in an eternal sunrise.

Clear as the mountain-peaks (O many-mountained
Hellas!) soar in the morning splendour
When the valleys below them drowse in shadow,
Those voices into the light uplift us.

Now in the hour of menacing malignity
Hellas, holding the ancient passes
Stands for the world's cause, knowing it invincible,
Knowing that beside her stand the Immortals.

Laurence Binyon

November, 1940

SALUTE TO GREECE [1]

What is Greece to us now?
How do we stand
to the little land
under the German plough?
Harrowed, broken, what is she worth to-day?
'Greece,' what does the word convey?

[1] Copyright, 1942, by Winifred Ashton.

Greece and Britain! Each is a little land
rocked by the mastered sea.
Each has bred a people whose sole desire
is to be free;
but hers is the older fire.

Remember the gods of Greece,
and how the Grecian women bore them sons
to slay the evil beasts,
pull down adulterous Troy,
bring home the Golden Fleece!
Remember the beautiful ones,
the goddesses Fortitude, Wisdom, Grace,
and how, in the age of gold,
Valour guarded the race,
and the nurse was Art!
Think of the songs at their feasts!
Think of the tales they told,
and how in gold and ivory dreams were wrought
by the free in body, the free in heart.

These made Greece the world's delight
until the Roman came
to bow her neck.
But he could not check
her bright and heretic laughter,
nor quench her flame,
till after, always after
the Roman, hurried the Hun,
to rape and mangle and maim.

A thousand miles away,
we too were overrun

by Roman and German, and fought
alone for liberty, counting the cost.
How should we know
a thousand ignorant years ago
of the free land where liberty was lost?
But in our own hey-day
out of Byzance
across the Alps and drifting over France
came rumours of a wisdom and a song,
Greek dance, Greek play
buried and lost — how long?
Then from the dust arose
Greece, and came forth
stammering: 'Liberty!'
Back to her place she goes
among the states where none is old as she
and none so young.

But what is Greece to us, now
that the Romans return
with the Hun?
Down from the stolen North
the apes of the barbarous forest are coming,
roaring and drumming
to plunder and burn,
profaning Olympus with dung.
How shall we praise the little land
under the German plough?

When a man passes the River,
and comes to be judged by his gods
he must deliver,
or so it is said,
in round terms all he has done,

out of his own mouth earning
eternal life or death among the dead.
Now to the gods of all men comes the Hun.
'Is not remembrance mine
in Poland, Spain and lands between?
Who will forget my torments bold, obscene,
the pain, the filth, the burning?
Shall I not immortality put on?'
But ever the hand divine
points downward to oblivion.
Another takes his place.
'What claim to long remembrance? Speak!'
'None! None!
I lost my name and breath.'
'Where?' 'In the Pass,
the bloody Pass of death.
I think my father was Leonidas;
but I forget my name. I know I died.
The almond tree was blooming. My wife cried.
I know I am a Greek.'
'A Greek!' Oh wide
and wide the portal
opens upon that word! — 'Enter, immortal!'

Clemence Dane

DELPHI

For Greek Independence Day, 25th March 1941

The daisies are at Delphi now.
Who climbs the olive-shadowed gorge will pass
Myriad anemones that star the grass
With crimson and scarlet and the glow of Tyre

Richer than robes of priest or prince
Who trod the track long since;
And that gold filigree of the morning sun,
The silver dew, the silver on the bough,
Glint in the shadow as treasure in the recess
Of marble treasuries
That swung their doors of bronze to golden keys —
Safe in the precinct, in communion
Of all Apollo's tribes and holiness
Inviolate of his altar-fire.

Above the ruin of architrave and drum
From pillars prone, the crumbling tiers
Of theatre (soon some crevice will be blue
With rock-campanula, green with lizards some),
Spring's daisies glitter in the dew.
I marked them there when the oracle was dumb,
Hellas a memory of dead years,
And thought how reverend soil, how fateful breath,
To lowliest weed and waste will come;
Nor dreamed Apollo still
Could rouse his hosts to shield the holy hill,
Could lighten from his cloven peak
And from the navel-stone of Earth still speak
Of death for Freedom, of life in such a death.

But on this festival day
Hellas the free, the brave, the one,
Knows the twin eagles that engirdled Earth,
  Winging her ancient fame to east and west,
Here at Earth's centre newly rest: —
  Whither the tribes go up to praise and pray
In temple not of marble, not with gold,
But strong in the faith of old,

Athens and Sparta and all men true as they,
The Commonwealth of Freedom, that had birth
Here, and went hence to all beneath the sun.

Far off the anemones — but remembering
I cup dream-hands in the Castalian spring.
Earth's common daisies be my token
That the oracle has spoken.

                                    Oliffe Richmond

GREECE

May 10, 1942

We fidgeted. The school-clock drawled its chimes.
   How small we were, and how the master prated!
Outside the sun and sparrows filled the limes.
   No wonder that we thought you overrated,
      For that is what our cricket-captain said.

How could we grasp the splendid and remote,
   Or love your verse when scholars made it prose
To humbler souls who, getting it by rote,
   Looked up resentfully to classic pose
      And mocked the withered laurels on its head?

None taught us to imagine that beneath
   Such wealth of dust the ancient fire was burning,
That living hands would twine a nobler wreath
   For Greeks, who, strangers to the realm of learning,
      Had wrought a truer epic in its stead.

The old barbarian night had blotted out
  The trailing glories of your afternoon.
The world had other things to think about,
  And overlooked two thousand years too soon
    Part of itself, for which no heart had bled,

Perhaps gone dry through floods of homage paid
  — At youth's expense — to shining, squabbling towns
And Thought's foundations, which they somehow laid.
  'The Balkan Question' and the men in gowns
    Were unrelated! If your tongue was dead

Perhaps our heart was. We, the inky boys,
  Knew that we knew you not. Then new barbarians
Came with their Nordic Kultur and the joys
  Peculiar to the soul of utter Aryans,
    Bringing their Latin jackals to be fed

On you. Whereat more than the past arose,
  A nation brave and one beyond all dreams,
And so the more oppressed by jealous foes,
  Whose Reason needs must hate what it esteems,
    And long had loathed the ethics that you led.

Starved, tortured, massacred, have courage yet,
  Until the day of vengeance and release.
While men go upright boys will not forget
  Ever again the glory that *is* Greece,
    Ever while human blood is warm and red.

                                        Vansittart

STONES OF GREECE

Pure, cold beyond the dream of death or birth,
We lay in currents of the life of earth
Where nothing came to quicken, or pollute,
No, not the deepest-penetrating root;
No life we knew that ended or began;
Nothing we knew of change till we knew Man.

   In on our rest, through the unrestful clay,
Man, chief of all the restless, forced his way;
Upon our quiet dark he loosed wild light,
Changeful as he, that lost itself in night.
We learnt fast then; we learnt to know the edge
Of biting steel, compulsion of the wedge;
His cunning violence split our joints; his hands,
His puny hands, imposed on us commands.
We that had never stirred, moved when he bade;
He lifted us, he carried us, afraid
Lest we should crush him, yet with subtle skill
Made our vast weight subservient to his will.
All that we were was moulded to a plan
Making us partners in the life of Man.
He brought us to a world of sun and moon,
Of pregnant dust in crevices; and soon
Our very substance changed; changeless within,
Upon our surface grew a changing skin
That bloomed like flesh in fond response to light
And golden flushes stole upon the white.
We could not stay aloof; on every side
Life fingered at us, life that lived and died.

   Yet this, so far, was but the common lot
Of every block out of the quarry shot

To where the building grew; we for Man's art,
No common privilege, were set apart.
In us, that were before but living stone,
He mingled with that life life of his own,
We grew into his creatures — man and brute,
Immortal tramplings, wrestling, strife, pursuit.
For, though in stately ritual pomp was shown,
His theme was conflict: madness overthrown,
Reason victorious; each unchanging hour
Showed law triumphant over lawless power.

Unchanging, ah! Nothing we know of time,
But change we know, child of primeval slime.
Man that had fashioned us in noble joy
We saw ignobly lusting to destroy,
Yet lacking means, till at the last there came
Some roaring terror with a breath of flame,
And shattered us, who were the very soul
Of that most beautifully ordered whole.

And after that, our way of being changed,
From all we were, or had become, estranged.
Yet still with aching memory we crave
The place we came from and the place Man gave.
Light was life there; the light is drabness here
And quickens nothing; we dwell in a drear
Kind of dreamland. Faces come and go;
Men still point at us, yet too well we know
How little lasts of all the life that ran
Through us when we were fashioned first by Man.
They tend us here like cripples; there, raised high,
Fronting the elements, we dared the sky.

But now, what new degrading change is meant?
What fresh disgrace? what worse imprisonment?

We, stones packed under mounds of shapeless clay,
Lack even that poor counterfeit of day.
In the old world Man made us large and free,
Shaping an image of what Man should be
Beside those images of lawless force,
The ramping Centaur-shapes, half man, half horse.
Those were the enemy, a rabble crew,
Foes of the godlike, traitors to the true.
Ere he must undergo the mortal lot,
Man made us, lest his wisdom be forgot.
When we are seen, our silences proclaim
The maker's thought and his undying aim.
Why are we hidden? is some challenge hurled
Against all noble order in Man's world?
Uncover us; this is no hour to hide;
Our place is with our maker, and our pride.

Stephen Gwynn

WITHDRAWAL FROM CRETE

Doggedly,
Inch by bitter inch bought dear with blood —
They are withdrawing towards the dark wood,
And beyond, the height; and beyond the height, the sea.

What night is come
Upon the pleasant island once ashine
With fruited fig, sad olive and green vine?
How is the grove laid waste, its singers dumb!

Here where in shade
The shepherd tuned his pipe while all the rocks

Were whitened with the fleeces of his flocks —
Here hell is opened and the dead are laid.

Here where a breath
Would scatter oleander-flower and wake
The sleeping silver of a little lake —
Here lie the shattered wings of the fleet of death.

God be your speed,
Good gentlemen of Britain gallantly
Fighting your rearguard action to the sea!
God send you ships in your so-desperate need.

And we, your kin —
Let us be strong and stronger yet who see
Ruin come even unto Arcady,
The hollow cities falling from within.

Now let the past
Open our purblind eyes: let us be sure
That to be innocent's not to be secure
And to be weak is to be lost at last.

Though the sea burn
And the highest hill be levelled with the plain
And the heaped bones of the dead be dust again —
We will return, O Crete, we will return.

White shall they gleam,
The tall refashioned cities in a day
When we'll remember anguish passed away
As a dream and the dark shadow of a dream.

Audrey Alexandra Brown

*

X. POLAND

*

DAWN[1]

Come, Brother — forward in the dark! To what?
  We cannot tell. The sea-foam flecks the brine,
  But what may lie beyond that sea — what mine
May blow our ship sky-high, or in what spot —
We cannot tell.
              That roaring in the sky?
  An aeroplane is coming. . . . Friend or foe?
  We cannot tell.
                Come — forward! Steady — so!
No one of us but stands head up, chin high. . . .

The sea — and yet more sea. Land! Harbour. Men . . .
  But men who speak another tongue, and stare.
  Entrain! Entrain!
            To-morrow we are there:
'Mid Scottish heather, in a Scottish glen.

And then — ah, then! — the memory will stir
  Of distant, dear, familiar glenless plains,
  And in your ear familiar Polish strains —
The echoes of the song you heard from her
That bore you, in your cradle: Poland's call!
  Answer the call like soldiers, men! The song
  Is but another summons to be strong.
Stand to!
        It is the morning. Stand to, all!
                   Antoni Boguslawski

[1] Translated by L. E. Gielgud.

A PASTORAL FOR POLAND

Now have the cries of bombed and drowned
a gentle, elegiac sound;
rumor of grief and news of pain
drench the dull mind like autumn rain.

And now the innocent and wise
crouch from the menace of blue skies
till they lie broken, or in flight
towards the ignorant shield of night.

The burning forest of the nations
wheels under the constellations;
the iron birds roar the bomb-routes; deep
in the explosions children sleep.

Together in the cool of day
the placid, great-limbed beasts of prey,
strong at the twilight hour, and feeding,
rend the sweet flesh before them bleeding,

and formless forms in slippers and cowl
watch with the still, round eyes of the owl,
soar from the tree of faith to bless
the perfect act of ruthlessness,

and crickets ring the leafing fire
chirping with terror and desire,
and the rest, under the shadowed hill,
rustle and scurry and are still.

— In the exhausted hour of peace
whom shall we honor among these?
The martyrs bleeding by the wall,
the humble, who cry out and fall,
 and these are all, and these are all.

Clark Mills

WARSAW, 27 SEPTEMBER, 1939

Space long was ours, factories to frame our guns,
 In wealth, in wit we led, in labour lagged;
 To war's inferno so reluctant dragged:
Man and the mineral ours, Time was the Hun's.

Time now we have been given, by heroes bought:
 Yours, Poland, be the glory! you'd not yield
 Till early rain soddened the Flanders field,
Holding the foe till our defence was wrought.

Trumpets to-day! trumpets of augury,
 High hope for prisoned Norway, Slavia, France,
  Freezing with glances icier than their air
  The conqueror with aloof and haughty stare —
 Trumpets of triumph, trumpets of advance,
Poland, you gave us *Time* — and Victory!

Leo Minster

Warsaw, September, 1942

*

XI. CANADA

*

CANADA SPEAKS OF BRITAIN

This is that bastioned rock where dwell the Free,
  That citadel against whose front in vain
Storm up the mad assaults of air and sea
  To shatter down in flaming wreck again.

This, this is Britain, bulwark of our breed,
  Our one sure shield against the hordes of hate.
Smite her, and we are smitten; wound her, we bleed.
  Yet firm she stands and fears no thrust of fate.

Stands she, and shall; — but not by guns alone,
  And ships and planes and ramparts. Her own soul
That knows neither to bend nor break, — her own
  Will, hammered to temper, — keeps her whole.

She calls. And we will answer to our last breath, —
Make light of sacrifice, and jest with Death.

                              Charles G. D. Roberts

August 19, 1940

THE DEBT

Sitting here in the glow of my study-lamp,
              Warmed and fed,
I think of the rain-swept bivouac or camp,
Of the rolling, plunging deck of a slim corvette,
Of the diving-plane; and wonder about my debt
              To living and dead.

Boys I thought them, blithe and of careless port
        Now-and-again,
Deaf to politics, set upon fun and sport,
Taking their studies lightly, as boys will do
Before they are staid and wise — like me and you.
        But they were men!

Knowing the feel of Liberty, worthy and strong,
        Willing and free;
Making their choice with a smile and a bit of a song;
Marching, sailing, or flying suiting them well
So they might slay the Devil and ruin Hell
        Upon land and sea.

Now of these paladins gaily serving the King
        What can I say?
Neighbours of Death, ashore, a-sail, or a-wing,
While the screaming bomb rakes bivouac and camp.
— Sitting here in the glow of my study-lamp
        I can only pray.

J. E. Middleton

*

XII. SOUTH AFRICA

*

JAN[1]

Old Jan Smuts, who was numbered with the foe,
Riding through South Africa some forty years ago,
Mounted on his pony, with his little Boer beard,
Slim as his voorloopers, and a fighter to be feared;
Quick and cool in action, ever working to an end,
Paladin of Africa, in whom we found a friend;

Old Jan Smuts, who had always watched the Hun,
Rode von Lettow Vorbeck out of places in the sun,
Leading troops to triumph whom he once led by the nose,
Thinking for South Africa, as each new dawn arose,
Planning for posterity, that all men might be freed —
Thus we learnt to know him for another hour of need;

Old Jan Smuts bears a baton for his pains,
Holds high place in history — but Jan he still remains,
Brown and hard as leather, though his beard is turning white,
Bringing new commandos into Freedom's grimmest fight;
Out again in harness for his own unconquered land,
Spirit of South Africa, and Christendom's right hand.

G. D. Martineau

[1] Reproduced by permission of the Proprietors of *Punch*.

*

XIII. DUNKIRK

*

DUNKIRK [1]

Will came back from school that day,
And he had little to say.
But he stood a long time looking down
To where the gray-green Channel water
Slapped at the foot of the little town,
And to where his boat, the *Sarah P*,
Bobbed at the tide on an even keel,
With her one old sail, patched at the leech,
Furled like a slattern down at heel.

He stood for a while above the beach;
He saw how the wind and current caught her.
He looked a long time out to sea.
There was steady wind and the sky was pale,
And a haze in the east that looked like smoke.

Will went back to the house to dress.
He was halfway through when his sister Bess,
Who was near fourteen and younger than he
By just two years, came home from play.
She asked him, 'Where are you going, Will?'
He said, 'For a good long sail.'
'Can I come along?'

                'No, Bess,' he spoke.
'I may be gone for a night and a day.'
Bess looked at him. She kept very still.
She had heard the news of the Flanders rout,
How the English were trapped above Dunkirk,

[1] Reprinted from *Dunkirk*, by Robert Nathan, by permission of and special arrangement with Alfred A. Knopf, Inc.
Copyright, 1941, by Robert Nathan.

And the fleet had gone to get them out —
But everyone thought that it wouldn't work.
There was too much fear, there was too much doubt.

She looked at him and he looked at her.
They were English children, born and bred.
He frowned her down, but she wouldn't stir.
She shook her proud young head.
'You'll need a crew,' she said.

They raised the sail on the *Sarah P,*
Like a penoncel on a young knight's lance,
And headed the *Sarah* out to sea,
To bring their soldiers home from France.

There was no command, there was no set plan,
But six hundred boats went out with them
On the gray-green waters, sailing fast,
River excursion and fisherman,
Tug and schooner and racing M,
And the little boats came following last.

From every harbor and town they went
Who had sailed their craft in the sun and rain,
From the South Downs, from the cliffs of Kent,
From the village street, from the country lane.
There are twenty miles of rolling sea
From coast to coast, by the seagull's flight,
But the tides were fair and the wind was free,
And they raised Dunkirk by the fall of night.

They raised Dunkirk with its harbor torn
By the blasted stern and the sunken prow;
They had raced for fun on an English tide,

They were English children bred and born,
And whether they lived or whether they died,
They raced for England now.

Bess was as white as the *Sarah's* sail,
She set her teeth and smiled at Will.
He held his course for the smoky veil
Where the harbor narrowed thin and long.
The British ships were firing strong.

He took the *Sarah* into his hands,
He drove her in through fire and death
To the wet men waiting on the sands.
He got his load and he got his breath,
And she came about, and the wind fought her.

He shut his eyes and he tried to pray.
He saw his England where she lay,
The wind's green home, the sea's proud daughter,
Still in the moonlight, dreaming deep,
The English cliffs and the English loam —
He had fourteen men to get away,
And the moon was clear and the night like day
For planes to see where the white sails creep
Over the black water.

He closed his eyes and he prayed for her;
He prayed to the men who had made her great,
Who had built her land of forest and park,
Who had made the seas an English lake;
He prayed for a fog to bring the dark;
He prayed to get home for England's sake.
And the fog came down on the rolling sea,

And covered the ships with English mist.
The diving planes were baffled and blind.

For Nelson was there in the *Victory*,
With his one good eye, and his sullen twist,
And guns were out on *The Golden Hind*,
Their shot flashed over the *Sarah P.*
He could hear them cheer as he came about.

By burning wharves, by battered slips,
Galleon, frigate, and brigantine,
The old dead Captains fought their ships,
And the great dead Admirals led the line.
It was England's night, it was England's sea.

The fog rolled over the harbor key.
Bess held to the stays and conned him out.

And all through the dark, while the *Sarah's* wake
Hissed behind him, and vanished in foam,
There at his side sat Francis Drake,
And held him true and steered him home.

Robert Nathan

'THEY MARCHED OVER THE FIELD OF WATERLOO' [1]

They marched over the Field of Waterloo,
By Goumont and La Haie, and then fell back,
Forever facing front to the attack
Across the English bones.

[1] Reprinted from *The Nine Days Wonder* (John Masefield) by permission of the Author.

Westward, by Fontenoy, their ranks withdrew;
The German many bomb-bursts beat the drum,
And many a trooper marched to kingdom come
Upon the Flanders stones.

Westward they went, past Wipers, past the old
Fields bought and paid for by their brothers' blood.
Their feet were in the snapping of the flood
That sped to gulf them down.

They were as bridegrooms plighted to the mould
Those marching men with neither hope nor star,
The foeman in the gateways as a bar,
The sea beyond to drown.

And at the very sea, a cloud of night,
A hail of death and allies in collapse,
A foe in the perfection of his traps,
A certainty of doom.

When, lo, out of the darkness, there was light,
There in the sea were England and her ships; `
They sailed with the free salt upon their lips
To sunlight from the tomb.

John Masefield

DUNKIRK

So long as light shall shine upon a world
Which has a human saga for the lyre,
A pennant at a masthead left unfurled,
A name, a title to be writ in fire;

So long as there is drama on the earth
And the wild pulses leap to the grand themes
That dignify our voyaging from birth
To death along the highway of our dreams;
This name shall be the symbol for the soul,
A new Promethean triumph in defeat,
And find its place in the historic scroll
That lists the immortal stand, the great retreat,
Attending causes ultimately won —
Thermopylae, Corunna or Verdun.

E. J. Pratt

*

XIV. RAIDS AND RUINS

*

RIDING UP THE HILL

Ride up the hill a little, and then turn
To look on the destruction. You will see
Poor Shakespeare with a bullet in his throat;
And a scarred Cross, the relic of a Faith.

All will be silence in your solitude;
The last child dead, the mutilated woman
Huddled and motionless. You knew that woman.
She was the mother of a million men.
A million more lie cheated in her womb.
She's fallen amongst the wild flowers, near the child,
The generation of spring, the fragrant carpet
Of hope, old earth's reassurance of life.

It will be best to hope. You should stoop down
And pick a primrose splashed with human blood,
And set the symbol in your bandolier
Just where the tunic gapes above the wound,
The wounded mind that will forever bleed,
Forever drain you of the power to love
Or cherish anything for more than a day.

That will not matter. Your generation knows
The worst that can befall the race of man.
You have seen his work, his best; and you have seen
Poor Shakespeare with a bullet in his throat;
Your son, your mother flung into the dust;
All general glory and all private treasure
Tossed out, and trampled on, and done to death.

Ride on, my brother, still higher up the hill.
Then look again, and tell me what you see.

Richard Church

ENGLAND — JUNE, 1940

The fields are bridal, flushed with dewy light,
England lies smiling through her maze of tears;
Nature is lord of day as Man of night;
Her beauty calms, he dominates by fears,
Anguish, oppressions, and the terrible might
Of evil forces bursting through the chain
Of spiritual powers given to protect
The gracious gateways of the human soul.
Great sorrows wander like wind-driven rain,
Destructions, exile, destitutions, pain:
Truths, tendernesses, pities all are wrecked
Within this hideous, widening battle-roll —
And yet Man's triumph lives: greatness appears
In every hour; it rises from the gloom
On wings resplendent with a bitter loss.
Nothing is now of pettiness or dross
But steadfast, silent payment, Freedom's price,
A resolution overmastering doom,
And warrior's crown of infinite sacrifice.

Gorell

CASTLE HOWARD

Castle Howard, in Yorkshire, where the writer spent much
of his childhood, was burned down in November, 1940.

This is the dream — this is the nightmare —
Here magic real, and the untrue true;
Wandering, wondering, past the stair
And along the passage as I used to do.

The garden-hall floor is warped and waving;
The dome is broken; the regular turning
Of rails round the gallery gapes; the paving
Is stained with tannin; and the smell of burning
Weighs on the air. Once with young yells
Through basement-passage, wheeling and whirling
On banking bicycles, braying our bells,
Went I and Christopher, before smoke came swirling.
We played in the hall with piebald paving —
Big-white, little-black, lines diagonal;
Twisted up the stairs to the dome, where raving
Flames in November burned it all.
In the dining-room where I the Papist
Was given poached eggs for Friday lunch,
The ice-wild wind is driving the latest
Quivering snowflakes, soft for the scrunch
Of the workman's hobnails. The sturdy walls,
Raw-red and charred, robbed of ornament,
Whipped and scoured by the razor squalls,
Grin all toothless, with cracked cement,
As dying men grin, leering madly;
This is the end of a phase, of an era;
The bricked-up doorway in the passage sadly
Marks the end of a stage, as the next comes nearer.
This is the forward step, with no backsliding;
The young days are bricked-up behind the wall;
Gone are the days when I came riding,
The hopefully hopeless good-bye in the hall.
The workmen who wheel the barrows of rubble
Out of the way to the wind-whipped garden,
Rake out the wreckage of a life without trouble,
Force me firmly where my soul must harden
Or be battered. There are memories of naked bathing —
Fauns in the fountain, of defiant lunge

At the terrace statue, of picnics in swathing
Bracken on birthdays, with Tilda's plunge
After riddle-running rabbits in the hot sun,
Of fly-buzzing bracken, of shadowed Temple Hole,
Of playing in the hay, of warm wet fun
During battles on the lake in canoes which roll.
That life is over, that phase has passed,
Bricked-up and sealed by the nightmare-burning;
I'm faced forwards, away from the past,
Forced forwards with no more turning.

Lawrence Toynbee

VALSE DES FLEURS

The house is in disorder
the chairs turned, the tables up,
the wallpapers wet and soiled
peeling in strips and hanging

on the floor are broken foods
and the damp, dead, unnameable things
are cast in disorder on the surfaces
while the windows reflect nothing ...

a strange house to come
after the dreams, after the hopes
after the leap into darkness
with the wet sands piled in corners

there are many rooms like this
dedicated in unconscious agony here
to those who dreamed infinity

to those who believed the essence
and thought from the wet deadness
she would lift them into space
out of the dream conception

there are many rooms like this

dedicated in the wilderness
baptized in sordidness
proclaimed by millions from the towers
and shouted forth in the loneliness

and I have lingered there
touched nervously the hanging paper
avoided carefully the tilted chair
guided myself past the open doors

and found nothing to create a name
nothing to hold up as glory
save in the farthest corner of a room
an old man weeping
fingering sadly the broken semblance of a violin.

                                        Denis Hudson

ROOM UNDER BOMBARDMENT

Quickly, before the walls split, while they stand
Capture this room with a yet fluid hand —
Workshop, called living-room, where friends have slept,
Argued and eaten, corner crumbs unswept,
Chairs threadbare with much use, stamp the mind's eye
With a clear shapeliness. The nearing sky

Presses far autumn twigs against the glass
And beyond window-vision raiders pass.

Entering here, the heart is comforted,
But wrung with loss for children who have fled,
Young men in stiff strange uniforms, and one
A prisoner in despite.   Oh, English sun,
Which will smile veiled and mocking on this plaster
Even when all is rubble of disaster,
Linger a little moment and define
The coloured books, the friendly lamp, the wine
Spilt on the rug; for words may be the sole
Relic and souvenir of this room whole.
Streak the white papers on the desk with light
Before the violent darkness which is night.
Destroyed, what can restore this room, rebuild
The comradeship once sheltered, true friends killed,
Children so grown that they are scarce the same,
Lost shabbiness, the shadow of a name?

Quickly, before the walls split, leave a mark
Of shape and feeling for the broken dark.

Phyllis Allfrey

LONDON, 1941

Half masonry, half pain; her head
From which the plaster breaks away
Like flesh from the rough bone, is turned
Upon a neck of stones; her eyes
Are lidless windows of smashed glass,
Each star-shaped pupil

Giving upon a vault so vast
How can the head contain it?

The raw smoke
Is inter-wreathing through the jaggedness
Of her sky-broken panes, and mirror'd
Fires dance like madmen on the splinters.

All else is stillness save the dancing splinters
And the slow inter-wreathing of the smoke.

Her breasts are crumbling brick where the black ivy
Had clung like a fantastic child for succour
And now hangs draggled with long peels of paper,
Fire-crisp, fire-faded awnings of limp paper
Repeating still their ghosted leaf and lily.

Grass for her cold skins' hair, the grass of cities
Wilted and swaying on her plaster brow
From winds that sweep along the streets of cities:

Across a world of sudden fear and firelight
She looms erect, the great stones at her throat,
Her rusted ribs like railings round her heart;
A figure of dry wounds — of winter wounds —
O mother of wounds; half masonry, half pain.

                                        Mervyn Peake

*

XV. KEEPING THE SEAS

*

TO THE SEAMEN [1]

You seamen, I have eaten your hard bread
And drunken from your tin, and known your ways;
I understand the qualities I praise
Though lacking all, with only words instead,

I tell you this, that in the future time
When landsmen mention sailors, such, or such,
Someone will say, 'Those fellows were sublime
Who brought the Armies from the Germans' clutch.'

Through the long time the story will be told;
Long centuries of praise on English lips,
Of courage godlike and of hearts of gold
Off Dunkerque beaches in the little ships.

And ships will dip their colours in salute
To you, henceforth, when passing Zuydecoote.

John Masefield

THE BOY

Taking his trick, the crew being at their meal,
The hefty skipper of the little craft
Kept a zig-zagging course; and quietly laughed
With chuckling grunts to think that ever he
Should come to steer a ship so crazily —
When something crashed; and instantly the wheel

[1] Reprinted from *The Nine Days Wonder* (John Masefield) by permission of the Author.

Was wrenched from out his grasp; and he was flung
Beneath the shattering wheelhouse — consciousness
Blacked-out . . . and, battering his brain, a peal
Of clashing bells that in his stunned head swung . . .
His troubled fingers in a numb distress
Still fumbling for the spokes. . . . And then again
Recovering his senses, he could feel
A dull ache in his fractured legs that lay
Crushed under tumbled sandbags; while quick pain
Searched through his vitals as he strove to rise.
And now with sickening certainty he knew
His eyes looked on the light of their last day,
And that his trim and handy little ship
With broken back had ended her last trip,
Scuttled by a torpedo: then his eyes
Gazed up at the scared faces of the crew
Gathered about him, working desperately
For his release: and, cursing heartily,
He ordered them to quit their foolishness
And not waste precious time; but launch the boat
And save themselves before the *Sally* sank.
Reluctantly in bitter black distress
They turned to leave him; and his brain went blank
Again — and peacefully he seemed to float
Borne on a sea of waveless lucency
Over the verges of eternity —
Till, sense requickening once more, he heard
The lacerating yell of a scared bird
Shrill in his ear; and, glancing towards the bow
With anguished eyes, he saw the waves were now
Brimming the bulwarks, and the ship about
To take her final plunge; and then he felt
His shoulder clutched; and knew still someone knelt
Struggling to free his helpless bulk in vain:

And, turning in red anger, rasped with pain,
Ferociously he glared in the boy's eyes
That looked in pity on him. With a shout
He cursed the fool, and vainly strove to rise
To teach the silly lubber to obey
His orders without question — roaring 'Go,
You blasted timber-skull!' But with a slow
And quiet smile the youngster stammered 'Nay,
Not without you, Sir!' With a wincing grin,
The skipper muttered: 'So, you reckon I'm done,
And think you can defy me? Well, we'll see —
Ay, we shall see, you snivelling whelp of sin!'
Then, as the boy still stayed, more tenderly
He murmured, gasping, 'It's just crazy, son —
A lath like you, to hoist a hulk like me!
Quit fooling now, you . . .'
       With a sudden list
The *Sally* settled; and the waters hissed
And gurgled, closing over them, as they,
Clasped in each others' arms, with bubbling breath
Sank in mid-ocean's all-devouring death.

         Wilfrid Gibson

TRAWLERS [1]

Dawn squall raking the harbour, an east wind's whistle,
Sleet on the skerries, the morning barely alight,
And a whisper running along the quays: 'The *Thistle* —
She hasna come hame the night.'

Three little trawlers berthed 'longside the jetty
While the sea-wet fish are flung on the rain-wet stone;

[1] Reproduced by permission of the Proprietors of *Punch*.

Bruceland, Hope o' the Morning, Annie and *Nettie,*
But *Thistle*'s away — alone.

Men in jersey and sea-boots, smoking and staring,
Saying but little — for what is there left to say?
A skipper shaking his head, a skipper swearing,
And — on with another day.

'Sandy!' says one — and spits — 'My ain gude-brither.'
'Jock!' says another. 'Aye, Jock was a dacent lad.'
'Wee bit Alfie — an' wha's t' tell his mither?'
'*Thistle!* ... It's bad, it's bad.'

Never a gun had she, but she sailed undaunted,
Knowing her risk and taking it fair and free.
Mines and Messerschmidts? Havers! the fish were wanted,
So the *Thistle* put to sea

And went her ways till the Heinkel stooped upon her,
Went her ways till the bombs and the bullets fell ...
Whispers along the quayside — '*Thistle*'s a goner ...'
Ah, but she went out well!

Doing her job. Let the tale of her fame go soaring
To those high halls where the sea-lost heroes bide;
And — 'Davie! Keep up yer fires an' t' hell wi' Goaring;
We're out wi' the evenin' tide.'

Our turn next? And it's no good watching and wishing.
Our turn next? And it's catch as the catcher can.
But — who looks landward? Who forsakes the fishing?
Nobody. Not one man.

Hilton Brown

ATLANTIC

No season frontiers here: the snow-white foam
   Expects no dark campaigning of the Spring;
No gold corn trampled; no long lived-in home
   Smoking in ruins, a tear-pictured thing.

Here bitter war has no such weeping; loss
   Is borne unseen, and gain goes unrenowned.
The convoy to safe harbour wins; no cross
   Marks where the ship was sunk, the sailor drowned.

                        G. Rostrevor Hamilton

SAILORS

From Beaulieu down to Brixham town
We sailed the summer seas;
We beat and ran and took delight
In every slant of breeze,
And one great star-beleaguered night
The dimming coast with lamps grew bright
Like fallen stars, and with delight
We sailed the summer seas.

You steer by Mars and foreign stars,
As I sit on the shore
And watch a convoy outward bound
Of forty ships or more
To deeps where men are bombed and drowned
And blown to dust — I see them crowned.
From Avalon still outward bound,
As I sit on the shore.

But someday yet our sails we'll set
And out again to sea,
And make our play with wind and tide
Where all that company
Of gallant men has fought and died —
Will they not frolic at our side
And take the tiller down the tide
And out again to sea?

Patric Dickinson

XVI. THE FLYERS

*

XVI. THE FLYERS

*

TO POETS AND AIRMEN

Dedicated to Michael Jones in his life, and now in his memory,

Thinkers and airmen — all such
   Friends and pilots upon the edge
Of the skies of the future — much
   You require a bullet's eye of courage
   To fly through this age.

The paper brows are winged and helmeted,
   The blind ankles bound to a white road,
Streaming through a night of lead
   Where cities explode.
   Fates unload

Hatred burning, in small parcels,
   Outrage against social lies,
Hearts breaking against past refusals
   Of men to show small mercies
   To men. Now death replies
Releasing new, familiar devils.

And yet, before you throw away your childhood
   With the lambs pasturing in flaxen hair,
   To plunge into this iron war,
Remember for a flash the wild good
   Drunkenness where
   You abandoned future care,

And then forget.. Become what
   Things require. The expletive word.
   The all-night-long screeching metal bird.

And all of time shut down in one shot
   Of night, by a gun uttered.

Stephen Spender

HARBOR VIEW [1]

Here where the gulls and the pilots fly
The accent seems to be on sky,
Not on the land which lies as flat
As a spatulate tongue in the harbor's mouth
Between its tall-toothed building jaws.
It looks old-fashioned lying there,
Grounded, with everything flying by
In the newfoundland, the land of air.

An airport beacon's swinging beam
On an arc of blue with the ceiling zero
Cuts a pivotal Milky Way;
And lights on a fuselage, red and green,
Shine like Aurora Borealis,
Only more brilliant, more cuttingly keen,
For the night to catch in her streamlined chalice.

Below in the darkness the ancient sea
Laps at the walls of the Battery,
Now no longer fortified,
For there has risen a stronger tide
Not stemmed nor stopped by any shore,
Nor windy strata, low or high.
The world today is a world of sky,
And the nebular outposts must be manned.
There is more sky than sea.
There is more sky than land.

Frances Taylor Patterson

[1] Reprinted from The Yale Review, copyright by The Yale University Press.

HYMN FOR THOSE IN THE AIR

To The Royal Canadian Air Force

Eternal Father, by whose Might
   The firmament was planned,
Who set the stars their paths of light,
   Who made the sea and land,
Thou who art far, yet near,
   In the bright Now and Here,
And where the Void is sleeping,
   Take them who dare to fly
Into Thy keeping.

Guide them who move through dark and cloud,
   Parting the pathless sky,
Sustain them when the storm is loud
   Till night and storm are by;
Driving through snow and sleet
   When wild the head-winds beat,
Thy sovereign Will commanding,
   Bring them who dare to fly
To a safe landing.

Lead them who, dauntless, mount the height
   Of the embattled air,
Through piercing shell, through searching light,
   Hold and be with them there;
Keep them in life or death
   Mindful of One who saith,
Where the wild birds shall gather
   Not the least sparrow falls
Without the Father.

Lift up the souls who yet aspire
  To move within Thy Will,
Who rise above the World's desire,
  Foiled but unconquered still;
Triumphant in Thy Might,
  Gather them into Light,
The Valiant who have striven,
  Winged with Immortal Joy
Into Thy Heaven.

Duncan Campbell Scott

HIGH FLIGHT

Oh, I have slipped the surly bonds of earth,
And danced the skies on laughter-silvered wings;
Sunward I've climbed and joined the tumbling mirth
Of sun-split clouds — and done a hundred things
You have not dreamed of — wheeled and soared and swung
High in the sunlit silence. Hov'ring there,
I've chased the shouting wind along and flung
My eager craft through footless halls of air.
Up, up the long delirious, burning blue
I've topped the wind-swept heights with easy grace,
Where never lark, or even eagle, flew;
And, while with silent, lifting mind I've trod
The high untrespassed sanctity of space,
Put out my hand, and touched the face of God.

John Gillespie Magee, Jr.

*

XVII. THE FALLEN

*

FROM MEN WHO DIED DELUDED

Written at the time Austria was taken over by the Nazis.

This is the time to speak to those who will come after,
To those who will climb the mountain-tops, although
The continual clouds have crept down upon us
And we cannot tell any more how far there is to go.

This is the time to set our lips upon great horns and blow
Far down the years a note to reach them when
They are failing on the crest before the end,
To fall on their ears like a sweet hail from men

Who did not reach so far but blessed their march,
From men who died deluded far below the peak,
The self-destroyed, unwilling, blinded, caught,
Yet who believed, yet who desired to speak —

Dying, to blow a horn for those who would come after,
Despairing, to send up one clear note from the edge of death
And as the victors falter to salute them proudly
With the hope we cherished with our final breath.

This is the time, this dark time, this bewildered
To give our mortal lives that the great peaceful places
May surely be attained by those who, when they falter,
Must be confronted by the living vision on our dead faces.

May Sarton

CAPTAIN COLIN P. KELLY, JR.[1]

Killed in action off Luzon, December 10, 1941

Alone, above Manila's bay,
A falcon on the cloudy height,
He hung, and saw the battered shore,
The stinging hornet-swarm, the tight
Encircling fleet, and answering roar
Of that proud rock, Corregidor.

One bird of God in that still air,
One call to heaven before he fell,
To strike one blow, and strike it true.
He drew his breath and made his prayer,
And said a long and last farewell
To all he loved and all he knew.

He saw the ship in her dark pride,
Haruna of the Setting Sun.
He turned his wings above the wave,
Struck like an angry hawk — and died.
And that great ship went down. No gun
Will ever speak from her deep grave.

God grant our deaths may be as brave.
                                        Robert Nathan

[1] Reprinted by permission of the author and *The New York Times*.

A SOLDIER [1]

There was a man was son and lover,
And he went soldiering the world over. . . .
O soldier, why so far?
Lovely and fair the home-fields are.

Little he knew of home and loving:
Gone as far as the wind's roving;
Unkindly tasks were his,
Shorter and sharper than a kiss.

Did he dream?　Was he ever wondering?
Silent he in the guns' thundering:
Oh, never a wild bird flew
More covetous of the things it knew;

Never a wave gave closer cover
To pearl and gold it pondered over
Than this man in his thought
Gave to his secret while he fought.

O soldier, why this reckless giving,
As love were naught and the joys of living?
Aye, life he gave as well,
Falling, and silent where he fell.

　　·　　·　　·　　·　　·　　·　　·　　·

There was a man was son and lover,
And he went soldiering the world over
Nor ever came again,
Nor with the plough, nor with the grain.

[1]　Reproduced by permission of the Proprietors of *Punch*.

In his lone bed out far, far yonder,
Did he ever dream, did he re-ponder
The lore of field and streams,
Fighting to save them in his dreams?

Oh, he went soldiering to his own knowing,
Like the rain's falling, like the wind's blowing,
Like the sunlight in the sky....
Lovely and fair the home-fields lie.

A. G. Herbertson

LAMENT

As I walked under the African moon,
I heard the piper play;
And the last place ever I heard that tune
Was a thousand miles away.

Far to the West, in a deep-cut bay
By the ceaseless sound of the sea,
We lived and laughed in a happier day,
Archie and Johnnie and me.

For they'd be piping half of the night
At every ceilidh by,
And I'd be dancing with all my might
As long as they played, would I.

Many a time we were at the Games,
And many a prize had we;
And never a one but called our names,
Archie and Johnnie and me.

But Archie's dead on the Libyan sand,
And Johnnie was left in Crete,
And I'm alone in a distant land
With the music gone from my feet.

> *I heard him under the African moon,*
> *That piper I could not see;*
> *Yet certain I am he played that tune*
> *For Archie and Johnnie and me.*
>   George Malcolm

Gondar, 1942.

'REPORTED MISSING'

From these operations one of our aircraft is reported missing.
— B.B.C.

When these the steely flocks of Death returning
    Dropped from the air, he did not follow them;
A farther journey than to Samarkand
    Or Sourabaya or Jerusalem

Drew his restless soul: with head held high
    He took the uncharted track that far outruns
The blazing speedway of the crazy comets
    And the stare of the incandescent suns.

Out where his course is set arise no cities
    Of man's devising, luminously pale
Under the ash-rose evening and the dark:
    Here cleaves no keel and here is bent no sail:

Only the airy strata, cloud on cloud
    Piled high in shadowy bank and shining whorl

Mimick cupola and towered bastion
    Built of the bright translucency of pearl;

And farther yet, beyond the bounds of morning,
    Far past the circling dark, lies like a sea
The unrippled deep on deep of clear gold light,
    The windless ocean of eternity.

Why should we mourn for him, who wears his strength
    Like a gay cloak he need not loose or shed?
Sorrow is our inheritance; he forever
    Is quit of our inheritance, being dead.

Silent are the purple hills of twilight
    But for one far faint bugle hoarsely sweet;
Vainly it cries to the unanswering dead,
    Calling the pulseless heart, the quiet feet.

Age shall not dim the glory of his youth;
    Time shall not frost his brow nor chill his breath.
He is free of hope and fear, he is free of living —
    And death itself has made him free of death.
                        Audrey Alexandra Brown

TAPS AT TWILIGHT

Memorial Day, 1941

Blow softly, bugles, for our honoured dead,
  And tell them, where they sleep through sun and rain,
The secret of their rest can now be read
  By us who know they have not died in vain.

Blow proudly, bugles, with a new-born pride
　　In our belovéd dead, who slumber on,
Still holding dear the Cause for which they died,
　　Yet died scarce knowing how the day had gone.

Tell them, loud bugles, we have heard the call,
　　The call from mounds where tender grasses creep.
If we break faith with them, we too shall fall
　　And we in unremembered graves may sleep.

So blow, brave-noted, through our ranks of doubt;
　　The goal is dim, the field is still unwon;
The night is dark, the hounds of wrath are out,
　　And a thousand terrors cloud the sun.

But blow, proud bugles, sweet and silvery soft,
　　And tell them valour walks their vanished world,
The torch their hands released is held aloft,
　　The riddled flag of honour floats unfurled!

Arthur Stringer

SLEEPING NOW IN COVENTRY

Here rests a lad
Whose idle feet
Strolled English lanes
With lilac sweet,
Sleeping now
In Coventry.

Here lies a girl,
Whose heart has known

The quiet of
An English home,
Sleeping now
In Coventry.

Here lies a man,
Hands gnarled with toil,
Who dug and delved
The English soil,
Sleeping now
In Coventry.

Here lies a babe
Upon the breast
Who scarce knew life
Ere it found rest,
Sleeping now
In Coventry.

Here lies a wife,
Whose loving fear
Mothered sons
All resting here,
Sleeping now
In Coventry.

O God above,
May they rest well!
Avenge for us
The dead who fell
Sleeping now
In Coventry!

Arthur S. Bourinot

DEATH IN MAY

Bury your love,
   Bury him deep in leaves,
   He is a fool who grieves;
There has been time for laughter,
   And time for sorrow,
   Full time to borrow
Delight of sunny days, delight of rain —
   Mystery of shadowed grass,
   Marvel of sunlit grass,
Strip-lights of green,
Broken by silvery sheen
   Of filigree dandelion balls....
He was young — he might come back to play
On such a day.
   O by his grave be laid
   In the hawthorn shade
Gold plate and cup —
Stretches of buttercup
   To hold sun's wine,
   And flat gold plates a-shine
Of the happy dandelion
   And speedwell's singing blue
   In grass the sun strikes through.
Then, if he should awake,
Eyes would their vision take
Seeing the plumed trees shake
   Round him again;
Ears would again employ
Breathings and hints of joy,
   Hearing the song of love
   Fall through the boughs above ...

O world that groans and cries,
Living by ancient lies,
He could your woes despise:
   And, when the mayflowers broke
   Along their boughs like smoke,
Out of life's dream he died
Into joy's living tide.

Muriel Newton

OFF DUTY

Fleet Air Arm

Far had he hurled his bomber through the sky,
And now, off duty, he could take his ease
And watch the warm, slow afternoon go by.

Within our summer camp by gleaming seas
We welcomed him — so simple, brave and gay —
The place was his whenever he might please.

There we would sail or swim, beguile the day,
And after tea, beside a driftwood fire,
Talk music, mountain-climbing, work and play.

'What is it like?' — we asked — 'your Highland shire?'
'Old moors and purple hills; glens thick with fern,
White hawthorn, woodbine and the wild rose brier.

'Blithe Alison, in spring, along the burn,
Makes haste to find her firstling daffodil . . .
War's a hard winter, but the seasons turn.'

Now twilight drew her curtains and we were still
Awhile, till all at once the wind had shifted,
Thin mist arose, the evening air grew chill.

He made to go. The ashen fire was sifted,
The foghorn echoed from the hollow shore,
The lighthouse beacon lifted, vanished, lifted ...
.   .   .   .

Even the eagle from his morning tor
Too wide an arc may trace, too instant soar, —
Crumple and plunge, and wing the sky no more.

George Herbert Clarke

IN A BRITISH CEMETERY OVERSEAS,
MAY, 1940

For you the lilac and the apple blossom,
for you the music of the nightingales,
for you the sleeping in the piteous bosom
of Picardy, at peace while all else fails.
Not yours to be tormented by misgiving,
to wonder if the sacrifice was vain,
to weigh the worth of dying against living,
now that the lunacy begins again.
And yet the valour free-born man desires
leaps to the heart in virtue of your fame,
and yours the spark from which undying fires
burst at the trumpet summons into flame.
Sleeping you fan them as with angels' breath,
from the hard-won immunity of death.

Richard Elwes

TAKING OFF

To die in spring, to join one's fleeting breath
With the uprushing breath of earth's release;
To go out into the sweet airs and the sun;
Distil, like scent, like sound, the essential self
Into the April winds; so to become
One with the rising sap, the unfolding frond;
To leave the husk of cold mortality,
Thrust forth one's spirit, birth-like, with the spring:
That were a time to dedicate to death.
To pass in that green season into silence
Is but a stopped chord, harmony resolved,
Music inviolate; or like a vision
Seen and with passion recollected:
Prospect perpetual of lovely life
Immutable in the mind, never bereft
Of beauty's flame in that survival brief.
No withering by insidious years, for those
That die betimes, of youth's ingenuous bloom;
No death, but a relinquishing of life
While ardent still it pulses, to inspire
A spring eternal, young as the robin's phrases.

Elizabeth Harrison

RECOMPENSE

Where lovely Avon winds her rippling train,
Jewelled with yellow lilies, through the lush
Forget-me-not-fringed banks — where the refrain
Of silver-throated lark and missel-thrush
Enchanted you, you will not walk again.

You will not see the fires of sunset burn,
And fade at evenfall, or hear again
The nightingale's ethereal nocturne;
And golden Junes will star the riverain
With fragrant flowers — but you will not return.

You will not see again the faery foam
Of blackthorn blossom breaking, when the Spring
Comes round again — and, in the falling gloam
Your feet no more will press the purple ling
That diadems the dear, green hills of home.

But, though your singing heart will never leap
With ecstasy again, in England's dower
Of deathless loveliness — this thought I keep:
You shared the glory of her greatest hour
Before your eyes were shuttered in long sleep.

Agnes Aston Hill

*

XVIII. THE DICTATORS

*

DICTATOR'S HOLIDAY [1]

A.D. 1490

Round the foot of Amiata, like a bride,
   Her silver train of olives sways unrolled.
Next, the dark chestnuts drape the mountainside;
Beeches above them, green for Eastertide;
   Highest, the yellow broom — her crown of gold.

Round that lone crest the world's infinity
   Lies dreaming in the lazy spring sunshine —
The far-off glitter of the Tyrrhene Sea,
The beetling rock of Radicófani,
   The Umbrian and the Tuscan Apennine.

Then, through the April hush, a roll of thunder.
   Down through the broom, the beeches' young-leaved glory,
Down through the chestnut-glades, the olives under,
Bounds a vast boulder, snapping trunks asunder,
   Towards Abbadía di San Salvatore.

A cottage bars its way; with one wild leap
   The monster butts it headlong, lengthens stride,
Crashes through corn and vineyard — hoarse and deep
The watching peasants curse, their women weep.
   Then — a new rumble down the mountainside.

For on that crest — red feather and purple hose —
   Siena's lord, Petrucci, sits sublime,
Smiling to see his mercenaries' blows
Crack loose a huger crag. It goes, it goes!
   The Masters of the World must kill their time.

F. L. Lucas

[1] Petruccio Petrucci, Lord of Siena, a typical petty dictator of the Renaissance, used to amuse himself by tumbling boulders from the top of Monte Amiata, to watch the havoc they wrought below.

LINES TO A DICTATOR

London shall perish — arch and spire and wall.
Thus you decreed. Her courts and gardens must
Be ravaged, and the insolent towers that thrust
Against your glory. Hovel and palace — all
Shall sway, shall tremble, till before the gust
Of your derisive laughter they shall fall,
And hope grow cold and pride be ground to dust
That once was sovereign and imperial.

So yesterday you spoke who had not known
That cities can be built by more than hands,
That spirit ramparts have more strength than stone.
Now fearful you look out toward Dover sands
And cry, amazed, 'The towers are overthrown,
The walls have crumbled — but the city stands!'
                                    Mary Sinton Leitch

*

XIX. THE CONQUERED

*

GOOD KING WENCESLAS LOOK'D OUT

Good King Wenceslas look'd out
Where the victors vaunted,
Death and terror stalked about,
Fear his people haunted.
No bells chimed across the snows,
Heaven and earth seemed sleeping,
But the sighs of watchers rose
And the sound of weeping.

'Bitter is the bread we eat,
All our fires are ashes,
Bondage know we and defeat,
Feel the tyrant's lashes;
Mercy of the wolf we plead,
Of the butcher pity,
See our murdered children bleed
In our murdered City.

'Tricked by foe and sold by friend,
Sentenced to subjection,
Must this be our story's end
Stripped of all protection?
Must we sink in slavery
Saint- and God-forsaken?'

'No, your living shall be free
And your Dead awaken!'

Sagittarius

E TENEBRIS

I tuned in to a symphony
from a conquered country.
They were conquered too, those violins,
and the wind in the reed was the wind of desolation
— out of the dark I heard the music come —
and the air in the pipe the air of the lost city
and the brass the cry of mutilation
and the silence its prayer for pity
and the beat of the drum the beat of the yielded drum.

It was grey music as all the streets are grey,
weary as feet are weary, uncomprehending
as sense that suffers the single day,
ignorant of its birth, unmindful of its ending.
It was a ghost that I heard,
the shadow of a wing across the sun
and the fall of a shot bird.

Yet those violins did more than play
their mock of music; over the heavy bow
and empty strings I heard them say,
'Though they have murdered their kin,
stronger than they, he shall not lie with the slain,
but his breath shall blow as the winds blow
across the reed and singing violin,
seeking his living symphony again.'

Helen Spalding

*

XX. INCIDENTS AND ASPECTS

*

REMEMBRANCE SUNDAY:
COOMBE CHURCH, 1940

Here we are on this afternoon of mid-November:
The quiet country church is well
Filled, but to-day there is no bell;
On one side the khaki ranks of the Home Guard,
On the other the bandsmen in their uniform,
And behind, the good country people warm in their Sunday best.
The squire is in his pew, the legion's banner laid to rest
Upon the altar where the candles burn
In the thin light of winter afternoon.

All is as it was before. A dream, a haze, a mist
Descends upon me and obscures my eyes
With the dear dead dust of centuries:
All is passing as it passed before
In days of the Edwards, Henrys, and Elizabeth:
The country folk come yet once more to commemorate their
           dead,
Singing, Onward Christian Soldiers, Onward as to war.
All is as it has been, as it was before:
So many wars, so many times
The bells ring out their chimes
For peace proclaimed, upon the village green under the elms and
           limes
That remember the faithful few
Who in every age do not return, their forfeit pay.

There are no bells to-day:
The sound of a plane passing overhead
Wakes me from my dream of the dead,
To find the parson ascending the pulpit,
His saw assuring us

Our cause is just;
We fight because we must,
We shall not sheathe the sword
We have drawn before the Lord.
He remembers before God the names,
The innocent country names
Of Bakers, Coopers, Smiths:
I see them early or late at plough
Against the clean, bare world of winter,
Or coming hot and sweating down the summer lane
From harvest, stopping at the brook
Among the water-cresses for a drink.
Now they are where there is no thirst, I think,
Nor any weariness, nor getting up from sleep,
Nor lying down at night beside their dear companion.
All that was fought for, all that they died for,
Gave up the dewy morning and the scented night,
The harvest moon, the stars coming out over the familiar hill,
All has to be fought for again —
The parson assures us their sacrifice was not in vain —
The price to be paid once more, in the lives of their sons,
While they sleep, those other ones,
Far away from Coombe, far from their home,
From the village green, and cricket in summer
And winter games among the trees,
In France, in Palestine, under the seas.

Fight the good fight, we sing:
The young airgunner with proud pursed lips
Carries the cross slowly down the aisle —
Fight the good fight with all thy might;
Christ is thy Strength, and Christ thy Right:
Behind him crowds the slow crocodile
Of bright-faced choir boys, newly washed and spruce —

Run the straight race, through God's good grace,
Lift up thine eyes and seek His Face.
So pass the singing men and at the end
An old and grey-haired clergyman
Weary with years, who has seen three wars,
Yet still keeps lively eye upon his flock,
His Oxford M. A. hood a little awry upon his back.
The people reverently stand as the procession goes slowly by
Singing, Faint not nor fear, His Arms are near,
He changeth not, and thou art dear.
The last light of the wintry sun lights up the cross,
The white head of the clergyman,
Laying a loving finger upon them every one
As they pass slowly down the church
Out of my dream, and day is done.

A. L. Rowse

TWO CHRISTMAS–CARDS [1]

I

The seas netted with ambushes
And the sky falling:
Under that fiery rain
England is dying again,
Immortal and dying.
Look: vale beyond vale of vanished Englands.

The pilgrims to Canterbury
Ride by Kit's Coty House:
Someone before the Celt
Raised those great stones and felt
Securely immortal
Over vale beyond vale of vanished Englands.

Rain-loved Cumberland mountains
And the streams running down,
High sheep-runs by whom first claimed,
What poet in what language named
Glaramara
Before Wordsworth in his vanished England?

Lichen and stone the gables
Of Kelmscott watch the young Thames:
England dies in the storm,
Dies to survive, and form
Another and another
Of the veils under veils of the vanished Englands.

II

For an hour on Christmas Eve
And again on the holy day,
Seek the magic of past time,
From this present turn away.
Dark though our day,
Light lies the snow on the hawthorn hedges
And the ox knelt down at midnight.

Only an hour, only an hour
From wars and confusions turn away
To the islands of old time
When the world was simple and gay,
Or so we say,
And light lay the snow on the green holly,
The tall oxen knelt at midnight.

Caesar and Herod shared the world,
Sorrow over Bethlehem lay,
Iron the empire, brutal the time,

Dark was that first Christmas Day,
Dark was that day,
Light lay the snow on the mistletoe berries
And the ox knelt down at midnight.

Robinson Jeffers

AT THE MOON'S ECLIPSE

Now over most of living kind
Creeps the stealthy terror,
Sleepy birds and wakeful dogs
Tremble at the moon's error.

The full calm eye of night shuts to
With an evil lid,
Trees that drink in silvery light
Shudder, feeling it hid.

If I did not know the cause,
As trees do, I should do,
Seeing night's eye so dusked with blood
And shutting evilly to.

But I know this is a game
Of shadow and is brief,
A game foretold with exquisite
Exactness past belief.

Now over the much vaster round
Of the earth, moon's mother,
This night is full of creeping dark
Where brother slays his brother.

On the Volga, along the Rhine,
In the Solomons' day,
Steel and fire, whining death
Wipe all light away.

A thousand men who loved sweet light
Plunge into the dark
Where never moon nor sun will come,
Never the faintest spark.

And no one can tell when this shade
Will slide from lands and seas,
We small men tremble with the birds,
Sad watch-dogs, and the trees.

                    Robert P. Tristram Coffin

MARTIAL CADENZA [1]

I

Only this evening I saw again low in the sky
The evening star, at the beginning of winter, the star
That in spring will crown every western horizon,
Again . . . as if it came back, as if life came back,
Not in a later son, a different daughter, another place,
But as if evening found us young, still young,
Still walking in a present of our own.

II

It was like sudden time in a world without time,
This world, this place, the street in which I was,

Without time: as that which is not has no time,
Is not, or is of what there was, is full
Of the silence before the armies, armies without
Either trumpets or drums, the commanders mute, the arms
On the ground, fixed fast in a profound defeat.

III

What had this star to do with the world it lit,
With the blank skies over England, over France
And above the German camps?   It looked apart.
Yet it is this that shall maintain —   Itself
Is time,   apart from any past, apart
From any future, the ever-living and being,
The ever-breathing and moving, the constant fire,

IV

The present close, the present realized,
Not the symbol but that for which the symbol stands,
The vivid thing in the air that never changes,
Though the air change.   Only this evening I saw it again,
At the beginning of winter, and I walked and talked
Again, and lived and was again, and breathed again
And moved again and flashed again, time flashed again.

Wallace Stevens

EASTER EVENING, 1942

Is this the time to speak? Shall we tell the strong
What they already know? Or tell the weak
What not to fear? Divide the right and wrong
With the musical tongue in the poetic cheek?

Shall we lift up some outcry, when our fate
Moves on us like a hurricane or flood?
With a few syllables make more delicate
The spectacle of violence and blood?

No! There is only this. And no Tyrtaean
Sentence is worth the expenditure of ink.
We need no marching song, nor any paean,
Only reality in what we think

And the mere valor of the common man,
That always will continue and persist,
That can endure all grief, and knows it can,
And, till it wins, will not unclench the fist.

It is beginning of wisdom when we withdraw
From the pleasant places where all things went well.
That's over. We obey the ancient law
That teaches us to make strange Heaven in Hell.

Many are cowards. Many others lie.
The cowards must learn courage, the liar learn
Not to invent disasters in the sky,
Where, he has said, only cross planets burn.

'Not for some victory,' not for any race,
Or dull dominion of this world we fight,
But for all strength of thought, kindness, and grace
That made 'the feud with Chaos and Old Night'.

Leonard Bacon

FLIGHT [1]

Everything is in flight now, trees and men.
Leaves flying, a gale of gold, but the roads
Dull, streaming with fugitives, whose animal stumbling
Apes the fright, the monotony of dying.
The trains fleeing, the shiploads in full course.
In the thick of the night the engines, winged,
Over cities that cannot escape. By day the bright
Parachutes tumbling, spilling into the streets
Enemy milkmen, postmen, their packs filled
With mail for the anonymous and doomed.
Everything, everything flees: the impractical body
Flees from oblivion, and the mind from the mirrors
That image its dreadful night, and, too, the heart
From the sound of itself, a muffled motor, whose meaning
Nobody can guess. Everything is in flight —
Exiles all, without rest, of destination
More ignorant than over the marshes the wild geese flying
To a happier climate. To what end? Where?
The race goes on although the track is blind.
There is no turning back.

Babette Deutsch

MOONLIGHT

Time was when we were closer, Moon and Earth.
  I was still-born and silent, while you cooled
And came to Life. I watched you giving birth,
  And envied you — perhaps we both were fooled —.
Yet, though we drifted evermore apart,
  I was no stranger to your children's heart.

[1] Reprinted from *The Yale Review*, copyright by The Yale University Press.

Theirs was my hour. They craved the Moon's return.
   I was the friend of lovers. All romance
Flamed to my pallor. I disguised the stern
   And paltry sum of human circumstance.
I silvered slum and wilderness. The sun
Has never laved your sores as I have done.

And then the German came, and from the sky
   Slew babe and woman, mangled age and youth.
My light became my lovers' enemy.
   My sickle cleared the very heaven of ruth.
Men saw my face with horror, and between
My risings wished that I had never been.

Now I, your satellite, do thank my stars
   That I am lifeless. I would sooner have
No warmth at all than suffer total wars,
   No Man at all than Huns who rape and rave
And rack. *I* have no History to tell.
Their feet have never soiled my asphodel.

                                      Vansittart

DECEMBER DAYBREAK

   Shrill, a joyous scream
   Startled me from dream —
   Starlings in a stream
   Flying past the pane,
   Darkening its bleak gleam —
   Starlings roused to flight
   From the roosts of night
   By the blink of light

As day broke again
Over Salisbury Plain
Chilly and rime-white.

And, still drowsing, I
Watched them flutter by,
Screaming eagerly,
Far afield to fare;
Till at length the sky
Emptied, and the old
Misery untold
On my heart laid hold,
Wakened and aware
Of the world's despair
Icing it with cold —
As I recalled, even while that happy flight
About its innocent business passed from sight
Throughout all Europe in the morning-light
Men soared on heaven-ascending wings to fight.

Wilfrid Gibson

THE SENTRY

As the dawn flushes the vast desert-sands
Leaning upon his grounded gun he stands,
And idly thinks what they'll be doing now
At home. . . .
          His Dad, already with the plough
Turning the stubble of Long Acre — Ned
And Dapple in the traces; and in the byre
His Mother milking Rosemary or Bell,
Cowslip or Curly; while still snug in bed

Peter and Peg sleep soundly till the smell
Of rashers frizzling on the kitchen-fire,
Tickling their nostrils, rouses them. 'Twas well
For them, the lucky youngsters, they could sleep
With naught to trouble them but thoughts of school,
Nothing upon their minds, nothing to keep
Them wakeful through nightwatches in a land
Of stone and sand and naught but stone and sand...

But Dad and Mother, they'd be thinking — ay,
They would be thinking; though it would be hard
For them to picture him, who'd never seen
This world-without-end sand and rock sand-scarred
And scoured to queer shapes beneath a sky
Of aching fire, who only knew the cool
Green woods and meadows round the farmstead...

                                              Green!
If he could but refresh his tingling eyes
On green fields under rainy English skies...
Could watch the roach and pike in Harker's Pool
Beneath the overhanging willows dart
From stone to stone or through the Summer day
With noses pointing upstream gently sway
With flicking tails and quivering fins, until
Suddenly a big boulder seemed to part
In two, and soundlessly an otter slid
Into the pool without a ripple, when
They'd vanish like live lightning out of ken;
And he could only guess where they were hid....

But was this he — the lad who'd watched that day
Within the shadow of the ruined mill
Beneath the slanted willows drooping green

The sunlight on the rippling waters play
And those lithe quivering fish, and who had seen
The otter slide — he, who now watched alone
In a scorched wilderness of sand and stone
And sand and stone and naught but sand and stone
Until it seemed that he had never known
In all his life aught else but sand and stone....

Ay, Dad and Mother, they'd be thinking ... Hard
For them to picture him; but he ...
                                        And now
He sees again the slowly-moving plough;
And then his mother crossing the stack-yard
With brimming milk-pails ...
                              They'd be thinking, too;
And what they would be thinking well he knew.

                                    Wilfrid Gibson

THE COAST-WATCH

With tingling eyes he stares into the dense
And wool-white fleece of fog that hides the sea,
And harkens to the waves that ceaselessly
Scour the Northumbrian strand,
Until the murmurous monotony
Stealing into his blood lulls every sense
Into a trance-like daze through which he hears
The creak of oars in rowlocks close at hand:
And still in stupor like a man of stone
Who sentinels a dream-enchanted coast
He stands, sense-bound,
As, grinding through the shallow sand,

Boats run aground;
And instantly about him swarms a host
Of helmeted grey figures, armed with spears
And swords and targes.... Then the sound
Of his own rifle shatters in his ears
As in a panic he fires randomly
At those horned Vikings.... And the blind fog clears;
And once again he finds himself alone
Staring across an empty moon-glazed sea.

Wilfrid Gibson

THE REAPERS

O still, still, still
As I stand here, for one more moment a golden shudder
Glides over the landscape. It runs up over the hill

And pours its noiseless cataract over the maple trees.
It hangs suspended. It glitters upon these wet brown faces
And arms, and the dazzling sickle, and the sickled sheaves,

And the horses, and the maple trees. I watch them, but remain
Remote. I shall never bring good or harm to these flowering
Girls, or the golden-headed men, or the golden sheaves of grain.

The evil implicit in our age like dust falls everywhere.
Even in these flowing, flickering sheaves of wheat I see it.
I see it in the singing faces, I feel it in the August air.

For that is all our fever. It is a fever of the spirit,
And it lies deep. It will heal again, but certainly not soon.
We cannot localise it, we cannot even see or hear it —

The smart, efficient, petrifying flavours of our age
Lie scattered all around us, not only in the lies and bullets,
But here, in the hot touch of a hand, or the turning of a page.

And still, being young, being lucky, as I stand here and the
     maples
Gather the autumn stillness in their long, archaic arms,
And the horses scarcely move, and the wheat falls, and the
     ripples

Of a wild and timeless brilliance cover these faces, O still
For one more moment I declare that whatever is living is love,
In some way, however hidden; and I lean out, I fill

My eyes and ears with this so soon to be forgotten day,
I call out your name; but of course there is no answer,
It was only that, being lonely, there was something I longed to
     say.

And now the moment is gone, the illumination, the terror,
Have gone. Life lies below me as motionless and clear
And hard as the reflection of a crisis in a mirror:

And calmly I watch. I think, as I watch these sheaves of grain,
Stagnant, deserted, drowned in the blue summer twilight,
Of a time when grief will assume her lucid forms again;

I think of the little old men crouching beside the waters
And cursing, and the women passing with their vermilion bowls,
The stony silence of the sons, and the wailing of the daughters.

                                        Frederic Prokosch

THE CAMPAIGN

The snow falls silently through the unnatural forest,
Falls silently over the frozen brow and frozen hand.
They are terribly sleepy. But still their hard wet bodies
Move on and on and on over the frozen land.

They do not hear the rustle of certain forgotten moments,
The lamplight falling through the rain on the pear-tree and the
      pears,
The bells on a Sunday morning, and the sweet, solemn faces,
The sudden joy on a girl's face as she leans over the stairs:

They do not quite recall, for even then they did not notice,
That something precious had gone away, had quietly gone away;
The hand had grown unsteady, and love had lost its pleasure,
And the low call of beasts disturbed the calm summer's day.

They cannot possibly hear the ruddy approach of evening,
Or the horses and the naked horsemen approaching the stream.
Snow falls, and they cannot hear the tinkling teacup
Take on the oracular magnitude and anguish of a dream.

They pause. And now they fall asleep. A strange new power
Governs their lives, redistributing the happiness and the pain,
And the nameless longings which gave their lives a secret pat-
      tern.
Their destinies flow on and on over the frozen plain

Like waves over the sea. They sought, in this career of killing,
Escape from the hushed and paralysed career of the plants.
Snow falls, and the leaning bayonets are glimmering
In the firelight. They sleep. None hear the soft advance

Through the treacherous mask of the birches: the polar twilight
Has washed away the necessity for belief or disbelief.
These soldiers do not hear, winding stealthily through the
    forest,
The savage and irresistible footfalls of their grief.

Frederic Prokosch

THE MOON AND THE NIGHT AND THE MEN

On the night of the Belgian surrender the moon rose
Late, a delayed moon, and a violent moon
For the English or the American beholder,
The French beholder. It was a cold night,
People put on their wraps, the troops were cold,
No doubt, despite the calendar, no doubt
Numbers of refugees coughed, and the sight
Or sound of some killed others. A cold night.

On Outer Drive there was an accident:
A stupid well-intentioned man turned sharp
Right and abruptly he became an angel
Fingering an unfamiliar harp,
Or screamed in hell, or was nothing at all.
Do not imagine this is unimportant.
He was a part of the night, part of the land,
Part of the bitter and exhausted ground
Out of which memory grows.

Michael and I
Stared at each other over chess, and spoke
As little as possible, and drank and played.
The chessmen caught in the European eye,

Neither of us I think had a free look
Although the game was fair. The move one made
It was difficult at last to keep one's mind on.
'Hurt and unhappy' said the man in London.

We said to each other, The time is coming near
When none shall have books or music, none his dear,
And only a fool will speak aloud his mind.
History is approaching a horrible end,
As Henry Adams said. Adams was right.

All this occurred on the night when Leopold
Completed the treachery four years before
Begun — or was he well-intentioned, more
Roadmaker to hell than king? At any rate,
The moon came up late and the night was cold,
Many men died — although we know the fate
Of none, nor of anyone, and the war
Goes on, and the heart in the breast of man is cold.

John Berryman

1 SEPTEMBER 1939

The first scattering rain on the Polish cities.
That afternoon a man sat on the shore
Tearing a square of shining cellophane.
Some easily, some in evident torment tore,
Some for a time resisted and then burst.
All this depended on fidelity.
One was blown out and borne off by the waters.
The man was tortured by the sound of rain.

Children were sent from London in the morning
But not the sound of children reached his ear.
He found a mangled feather by the lake,
Lost in the destructive sand that year
Like feathery independence, hope. His shadow
Lay on the sand before him, under the lake
As under the ruined library our learning.
The children play in the waves until they break.

The Bear crept under the Eagle's wing and lay
Snarling; the other animals showed fear,
Europe darkened its cities. The man wept,
Considering the light which had been there,
The feathered gull against the twilight flying.
As the little waves ate away the shore
The cellophane, dismembered, blew away.
The animals shook, the Eagle soared and dropped.

John Berryman

CURTAIN

Goodbye.
            Incredulously the laced fingers loosen,
Slowly, sensation by sensation, from their warm interchange,
And stiffen like frosted flowers in the November garden.
Already division piles emphasis like bullets,
Already the one dark air is separate and strange.

Goodbye.
            There is no touch now. The wave has broken
That for a moment charged the desolate sea.
There is a word, or two, left to be spoken

— Yet who would hear it? When already distance
Outmeasures time, engulfs identity?

Already like the dreamer startled from sleep,
And the vivid image lost even in waking,
There is no taste now for the shrunken sense to keep;
And these, the dreamer's eyes, are not alive to weep,
And this, the clinic heart, the dreamer's, is not breaking.

Is it so easy, then? Goodbye no more than this
Quiet disaster? And is there cause for sorrow
That in the small white murder of one kiss
Are born two ghosts, two Hamlets, two soliloquies,
Two worlds apart, to-morrow?

Helen Spalding

MIGRANTS

Over the conquered countries
The southern birds go home,
Martin and swallow, fading
Above the Channel foam.

Eager with April faring
From valleys veiled with vine,
They saw in English orchards
The apple blossom shine.

Where by Sicilian temples
The lemon gardens glow,
Heedless of human heartache
The happy wanderers go.

Heedless of Greek and Roman
Who built those walls and died,
Their golden brief horizons
Are dawn and eventide.

Down to the conquered countries
Their cry comes, faint and far,
As they flash over, heedless
As moon and morning star.

Dudley G. Davies

REJECTED ODYSSEY

Can you not now remember
How we felt the limbs of the Downland
Stretching to rest
Under the green turf
With the chalk-white revelation of her breast
Through the blown garment of the grass?
Until in a dewpond
Night flashed a smile in an instant's reflection,
And we comprehended the intense face of beauty.
But you were afraid,
Self-clipped your wings
To find reassurance in people
And the dross of habitual things.

I wanted you to turn
And sail outwards with me
To a world I could not conquer alone
Save you stretched hands
To the ropes of my argosy.

We would have seen the shares of day
Ploughing the blue arable of darkness,
The sun flowering in those bright furrows
Unfolding and thrusting its pollen heart
To the high noon.

But the wine of a dying world
Runs purple and red in the beechwoods.
Earth curls her wintry lips to the falling treasuries,
Leaf on leaf, rustling and nestling to silence on her cheek.

The boulders of the clouds
Are rolling to their disintegration
In the splinters of the rain.
Fields lifting invisible mouths
Thirst, and are assuaged at the drench.

Why have you deserted these cities of earth and air
For the man-built huddles of security?
Were the cloisters of evening not sufficient for your contempla-
        tion,
Or the fountains of morning for your ecstasy?

John Perrin

TRANSCONTINENTAL BUS

On a strange land we have the light now, we are banked
In a light that plays with green like shimmering wings,
And like the shifting of the speeding land beneath us,
The conversation across the aisle drifts and sags —
The milk strike, price of grain, politics,
And the grim shadow of war, repeated war.

War is in every word, on every tongue,
In the clubbed newspaper waved for emphasis,
In the bus wheels singing: we are going east,
We are sawing away the miles, and as we grind,
The night that buries Europe is hurrying to us.
What have we with turmoil, I think, we in this light,
Surrounded by fields and orchards and breathing wind?
Are not the corn-flame, the trees enough for them
Through excited windows that they must speak of gas,
And force, and hate? Look to the sky and marvel!
But as I look, and as the road is torn by thunder,
I see the far shade, the setting sun behind,
And darkness sweeps in waves upon the world,
Pressing the fields, cutting the hills apart,
And drowning all our talk and eyes in night.
It is the night assailing us as ever,
Night in the east toward which the fast wheels spin;
Europe has had it; Europe sends it on to us
With choking sights within its eyes of stars
And thoughts in the dark wind that cool our words.

Daniel Smythe

REFUGEE IN NEW ENGLAND

Across the snow the water-color blue
shadows of woods ran out to meet the wall
crannied with whiteness; and the thin boy, new
to alien winters, watched his shadow fall
beside a pine's, and saw himself grow tall
in the wide sunlight where the rime-frost flew.

In these American woods there was no sound
save when a green bough slipped its load to earth.

Strange peace was here. Even the dog's bark, bound
hillward from the farmhouse, held a dearth
of urgency. The bright air flung its worth
upward: 'Oh, there you are!' — a friendly sound.
The young boy wept, his cheek against cold ground.

Frances Frost

FOR THE QUAKERS

Theirs is the gentle finger on the pulse
Of war's old woe.
Persistent, with the clear unrancored eyes
Of faith, they go
Where disillusion lost the charted way.
Unerringly
They reach across the desperate long miles,
The sullen sea,
And find the thin small fingers in the cold,
And touch, and hold.

Bianca Bradbury

ON THE FRONTIER

'Where is your home, Sir?' Such the question posed
    By bland official passing through the train;
Languid was I, disconsolate, disposed
    To take my ease and count my comforts gain
In the Americas. But, when he said,
    'Where is your home?', with kindling eye suffused
And heart a-sighing, lifting up my head,
    As one with sudden splendour all bemused,

'In England,' answered I. Straight fell away
  All languor, all soft relish. On thy brow,
O England, scarred and faithful, gallant, gay,
  Such coronal of glory wearest thou,
Thy wandering sons count each day life denied
Reft from thy pain, thy beauty and thy pride.

Nathaniel Micklem

FOR THE UNDEFEATED

Imperiled stands the day. Up the bright street
The shadows slowly creep and darken slowly
The sunlit pavement and the yellow leaf.
Windless, the trees are heavy in the air,
The flags hang silent, and the clouds come on
As imperceptibly as time. Dangerous
Are these approaching thunderheads and these
Attendant lightnings, and the night that falls
Unnoticed, terrible, in the heart.

In the city men walk with canes tapping
Like blind beggars, and the open windows
Bring in no light, nor do they throw the lamplight
Into the garden. Talk is in whispers.
We have locked our valuables away,
And forgotten how to spell in our own language.
Dust gathers on the piano and the violin case,
And when we kiss one another it is furtively in corners.

A bomb fell on the Museum among the Impressionists
And the plaster casts of Greek gods.

The librarian burned his books. The post office
Stopped sending letters except for the government,
And the radio stopped playing Brahms.
Night fell, and the doctor broke the test tubes in his laboratory,
The lawyer couldn't keep up with the legislature,
The Broadway stars went back on the road,
And the rain fell all night upon the city,
And the darkness over it was like mist.

II

Do you remember, Maximilius, the rain
Falling in Gaul, and the legions marching,
Footsore, south to the Alps and Rome?
Three weeks from home, Maximilius,
And the Huns behind us. Have you forgotten
The skins across their shoulders and the horns of deer
Stuck in their helmets, the great knives,
The war cries shrilling in the blood?
Rain was falling in Appia and the night
Drew down behind us as we fled.
Do you remember, Maximilius, the darkness
Gathering in Rome?

Have you forgotten, Crito,
The killing of brothers and the Thracian hordes
Walking within our temples? Do you remember
Dusk here in Athens among the olive trees,
Dusk in the markets, in the streets, between
The radiant pillars of the Parthenon? Crito,
Remember how the evening came and stole within,
Chilling as hemlock.

Do not forget, Atahualpa,
The Spanish horses prancing in the golden sun,

Nor the slaves bearing ingots for the conqueror.
Remember always in your heart, O King, the vines
Creeping among the caryatids of temples, the crumbling
Of the walls of Cuzco, and the black midnight
That seized you, strangling, here upon your altar.

III

Under our portals now the shadows lengthen,
And our fires turn swift to ashes. Into our keyhole
Seeps the ancient dust. What we have saved of silver
Tarnishes, and the towers we built to stand forever
Mock us. In our factories men put away their tools,
And we close our books, shut off the radio, eat
A last meal, for night has come.

But if night falls, believe me,
Dawn will return. If we must sleep
Let it be as children, dreaming of tomorrow,
Or as lovers sleep, waking in the night to rise
And go out into the gardens and walk
In darkness among the flowers, not seeing color
But knowing the rose also is awake.

And many of us, sleepless,
Will sit together through the long night, talking
Of friends remembered and dead poets and the earth
Warm in the spring between our fingers. Some
Will die in the slow hours of returning day,
Some have already fallen asleep never to wake, some
Will always sit patiently in the shadows waiting
For yesterday to return.

The darkness claims us.
Let us climb the hill and look for tomorrow.

We will sleep in the meadows where the sun,
Rising, may find us early. We will know,
Even in darkness, that the earth turns beneath us,
And we will dream of our seeds in the earth
And of the harvesting of them, and of the dawn
That will dazzle the treetops when we wake.

Eleanor Wells

THE REFUGEE [1]

In England, on the downs,
Where wild things fly and creep
Far from the noise of towns
And summer seems to sleep
And bells from distant sheep
Tinkle through dreamy air,
Only last August there,
In a chalk valley deep
Where went past elm and willow
And haunt of fox and hare
By wandering ways a stream,
Flashing its little billow
And fading like a dream,
There in a garden lit
By rays enchanting it,
Level and gold and long,
Gilding the midges' throng,
Where tall delphiniums were
And hollyhocks grew strong,
I saw a spirit sit,
Singing a doleful song.

Around her where she sate
More bright was every hue
Of flowers and grass, more blue
Delphiniums were, and through
The leaves the level, late
Rays shone more bright and all
Near her was magical.
Behind her a dark yew
Rose up. She was as tall.
I spoke and asked her who
Tended that plot so small,
Where she had come to wait,
So hidden from great things,
For she seemed something great,
One who might speak with Fate
Or mend the ways of kings.
And at my questionings
She turned and said that she
Now poor, was Liberty
And once had wide estate
And that her eastern gate
Was of old far away,
But, of her lands bereft,
This English garden, deft
With little paths that stray,
Was all that she had left.
Far through that garden lay,
Like some enormous oak
Felled by a lightning-stroke,
And left where weeds' decay
Covers it like a cloak,
A long mound on the clay,
Through which there flashed a ray
Which weeds could not conceal,

As though a thing of steel
Were hidden from the day,
Something akin, for wonder,
To hurricane and thunder.
And now the sun dipped under
The old down that I knew
And dim the spirit grew.
(The bees had ceased their plunder
And small birds homewards flew)
The spell was going too
That lately had enchanted
This spot the spirit haunted,
Where flowers of mauve and blue
And white and pink were planted
And, dazzling, dancing through,
The evening rays had slanted.
Now dim as though I dreamed
The fading spirit seemed
While flashes no more gleamed
From the half-hidden thing.
'Spirit,' I quickly said
As she was vanishing,
'What is in that long mound
Which weeds are burying?'
She spoke with scarce a sound,
But silence hung so dead
And heavy that I heard,
For now no more a bird
Or insect, even, stirred
And in that hush profound
She said, 'In English ground
Here I have hid my sword.
But I will go abroad,
To France, to France again,

And once more be adored.
Once more shall rise my star
Where the great clusters are
And I will travel far
With millions in my train.'
She vanished, and the heap
Where the great sword had lain
Seemed nothing but a steep
Long bank where ivies creep.
The hush resumed its reign,
And over down and plain
All nature seemed to sleep.

Dunsany

SPRING–SONG, 1939

Once more the woodlands ring with birds — but not to the birds
    men hearken.
  Spring like a bride comes bright with flowers — and yet the
    Spring's afraid.
Soon with ten thousand wings of Death shall the summer sun-
    light darken?
  Heart, you have heard the Spartan's word — 'We fight, then,
    in the shade.'

F. L. Lucas

STRATFORD UPON AVON

No more the stream is gilded
  With man's contrivéd light;
Down upon Stratford tumbles
  The old, unbroken night.

The chestnut's thousand torches
   But decorate the day;
No lantern guides the lovers
   Who tread the lightfoot way.

Still is the dark defeated
   By burning of desire,
The lover and the minstrel
   See all by secret fire.

So now, in blackened Stratford,
   Behind a roof and walls,
Shine yet the stars of Belmont
   And moon of madrigals.

No lamp illumines Avon,
   But flash of dancing phrase,
Where the poet is the beacon
   And every line a blaze.

              Ivor Brown

THE COST

It was a shabby house, lacking grace or dignity.
The professor's wife herself
opened the door, her dear remembered face
chiselled by destiny, a mask of fortitude.
We sat in a room bare and clean:
a deal table strewn with papers,
books on a home-made shelf
marked it the professor's study.
'Do you remember me, Madame?

You were very kind to me, years ago
when I was a student in Vienna.
Often I sat in the professor's study
drinking coffee, listening to his brilliant talk.'

  .   .   .   .

Professor Hartmann, eminent biologist,
was a great man in our student world,
his book-lined room a paradise, and Madame
the angel of our dreams. Pictures on the wall,
a cabinet of ivories, deep-cushioned chairs,
a leaping fire, coffee in thin china cups,
and little Karl passing the heaping tray
of pastries with solemn and joyful mien:
the professor in brown velvet smoking-coat
and tasselled skull-cap, fine cigar in hand
dominated the scene, illuminating with a word,
elucidating with a phrase, and always ending,
'The truth, gentlemen, whatever the cost, always — the truth!'
There was a weekly pfennig sweep
on the exact minute he would say it —
Madame at least must have noticed
how all eyes turned to the great gilt clock.

   .   .   .   .

'So you were one of those? My husband
will be glad to see you.' A small
flame of animation lit her voice. 'Have you heard
what happened?' 'No, Madame.'
She spoke without emotion:
'It was required of the faculty to teach
that German blood was of a different composition —
chemically different, you understand —
therefore the German biologically superior,
"herrenvolk" — a master race.
Professor Hartmann of course resigned.'

' "The truth, gentlemen, whatever the cost, always — the
       truth," '
I murmured. 'You have not forgotten?'
A brief smile flickered across her face.
'You lads had a wager on his saying that,
had you not?' 'You knew?' 'Of course.
But who could dream what the cost would be?
We were warned one day by a strange young man
who whispered to us as we walked in the park.
We dared not return to our house, but hid by day
and walked by night — and so escaped.'
After a silence I ventured, 'Your son?'
His mother's face was grey.
It flashed on me he might be dead,
or in a concentration camp. . . .
In brittle tones she said,
'His name may not be spoken in this house.
He is high in the councils of the Party.'
Her hand touched my arm,
light and dry as an autumn leaf,
her eyes pleaded for belief, 'I think
that it was he who sent to warn us.
Don't you think it was Karl
who sent the strange young man?
You remember how affectionate he was,
how gentle, and how kind?'

'I remember, dear Madame,' I said,
But I thought, 'I wish he were dead,
I wish he were dead.'

                                   Mary Elizabeth Colman

*

XXI. REFLECTIONS

*

THERE IS STILL SPLENDOUR

I

O when will life taste clean again? For the air
Is fouled: the world sees, hears; and each day brings
Vile fume that would corrupt eternal things,
Were they corruptible. Harsh trumpets blare
Victory over the defenceless; there
Beauty and compassion, all that loves the light,
Is outcast; thousands in a homeless night
Climb misery's blind paths to the peak, Despair.

　　Not only martyr'd flesh, but the mind bleeds.
There's nothing left to call inhuman, so
Defaced is man's name by the things men do.
O worse, yet worse, if the world, seeing this,
The hideous spawn of misbegotten creeds,
Grow used, drugged, deadened, and accept the abyss.

II

There is still splendour: the sea tells of it
From far shores, and where murder's made to lurk
In the clean waters; there, men go to work
Simply, upon their daily business, knit
Together in one cause; they think no whit
Of glory; enough that they are men. To those
Who live by terror, calmly they oppose
What wills, dares, and despises to submit.

　　And the air tells of it: out of the eye's ken
Wings range and soar, a symbol of the free,
In the same cause, outspeeding the swift wind.
Millions of spirits bear them company.
This is the splendour in the souls of men
Which flames against that treason to mankind.

Laurence Binyon

December, 1939.

THE FINE NATURE

This fine nature clear
Goes as a stream through brake and pasture,
Questioning not, disdaining none,
Fair friend alike of shade and sun.
We happening near
Are offered without any rumour or fear
A gentleness, a strength, the way
That first was meant the heart of man
Should go, when meeting the unsolved hours,
And so few can,
But this one counts the age in flowers:
So fragrance, colour, jewel, song
Attend along.

How great the miracle I find,
While all is zoned with thunder-smoke,
In such a constant mind —
Which, serious-playful as the brook,
And with like gift of beauty won
From stem or stone, from walk or run,
Amid my meadows cannot be
But ever kind and ever free.

Edmund Blunden

DISCOVERY OF THIS TIME

Not by the Poets.

Nobody borrowed a couple of dogs and a gun and
Packed out: keeping the evening forward:
Keeping the thrush to the left hand of the sun:
Following wandering water: building cover in
Four foot of wet snow in the underbrush:
Bringing the evidence back in a bag — a plover — a
Large bird: killed on the nest and no name for it.

No one set out for it. Nobody looked for the way here.

Not by Philosophers.

                    Nobody sat to a map of the
Whole world: measured the drift of the stars: of
Letters in bottles: figured the flight of the lapwing:
Marked the compass courses on the chart —
'Here will be islands.'

                    'Here will be those shores.'

'Coast will show here where the dolphins are.'

Nobody figured it out on a fine morning
Propped on a wine-butt by a windy sea
With a lit pipe and a lead stub and a board's end. . . .

(And they sailed and there was log wood on the sea.)

Not by the Conquerors either.

                              Nobody led us here,
Nobody lined us up in a town field:
Shipped us in barges: fought at the stormy head:
Marched on for three days in the desert:
Encountered the elephants: beat them; buried the dead in a
Closed ring:
                    And the next night to the west of us
Sea gulls over the sand: the wings numberless.

There are Leaders enough and they say what a mouth says but
None of them led us here!

                         No man beat the drum ...
Trekked to the site of it ...
                              Marked the shore and the harbors ...

We came by ourselves.

                         We looked and we had come.
There was one day and we walked from our lives and we stood
          here.
There was one day and we moved out — the neighborhood
Selling the farms: leaving the stock in the paddock:
Leaving the key in the lock and the cake on the table:
Letting the door slam: the tap drip ...

There was one day and we looked and we had come here.

No one discovered it. No one intended it either.
There were all of us — all together — and we came.
                                        Archibald MacLeish

THE WAR GOD

Why cannot the one good
Benevolent feasible
Final dove descend?

And the wheat be divided?
And the soldiers sent home?
And the barriers torn down?
And the enemies forgiven?
And there be no retribution?

Because the conqueror
Is an instrument of power,
With merciless heart hammered
Out of former fear,
When to-day's vanquished
Destroyed his noble father,
Filling his cradle with anguish.

His irremediable victory
Chokes back sobbing anxiety
Lest children of the slain
(When the ripe ears grow high
To the sickles of his own
And the sun goes down)
Rise in iron morning
To stain with blood the sky
And avenge their fathers again.

His heart broke before
His raging splendour.
The virgins of prayer

Fumble vainly for that day
Buried under ruins,
Of his pride's greatest murder
When his heart which was a child
Asking and tender,
He hunted and killed.

The lost filled with lead
On the helpless field
May dream the pious reason
Of mercy, but also
Their eyes know what they did
In their own proud season,
Their dead teeth bite the earth
With semen of new hatred.

For the world is the world
And not the slain
Nor the slayer, forgive,
Nor do wild shores
Of passionate histories
Close on endless love;
Though hidden under seas
Of chafing despair,
Love's need does not cease.

                                    Stephen Spender

READING GIRALDUS CAMBRENSIS

Look at the peace of inanimate things,
The sanity of stones,
The probity of pasture fields, dead trees,
Old hills, and patient bones.

Giraldus tells us the Archbishop stood
To preach at Parc-y-cappel
'On a verdant plain' — wherefore the people
Built there a chapel.

This bishop in 1188
Preached them the third crusade.
(A footnote adds that 'Chapel Field' now marks
The sermon that he made.)

Think, when at Parc-y-cappel, what young Taffy
Here took the Cross.
Did he sing, marching Europe, sad Welsh hymns
And look at a loss?

Think of that stream of miserable men,
The half not knowing
Where with their mormals, sags and wretched staffs
They were meekly going.

Think of the Sickness of the Hoste, the famine,
The ant-like army's woe:
Betrayed by leaders, knackered by black Arabs,
Eight hundred years ago.

The sorrow-serpent wound by that Archbishop
Has wound away in pain —
But Chapel Field, now churchless, is once more
A verdant plain.

Look at the peace of inanimate things,
The sanity of stones,
The probity of pasture fields, dead trees,
Old hills, and patient bones.

                                        T. H. White

THE WAR IN THE DARK

*— Sir, in my heart there was a kind of fighting
That would not let me sleep.*

This fighting grows more hideous hour by hour:
Who can be brave against the war in the dark?
Whose wisdom taut enough to generate light?
Harsh conscience, stifled heart, no help at all;
Night without comfort, winter without sleep,
Nervousness rife, love perishing in cold.

Hell is an agony of bitter cold
Whose fang corrodes, whose talons fix the hour
On frozen rigid points, impaling sleep
Forever out of reach, and turning darkness
From time to permanence, infecting all
With chill and idiot doting, void of light.

Illumination or illusion, light
Fails, and is gone, and, residents of cold,
All we can do is hurt each other always,
Improving on our methods every hour,
Struggle, embracing, locked and tight, in dark
Never succeeded, as it was, by sleep.

There used to be a certitude that sleep
Would be a preparation for the light
Of morning, and the day, however dark
The weather, and the year, however cold,
Would yield their season of armistice, their hour
Of decent mercy, compassionate for all.

But now the singers and the dancers all
Are still as stone, and neither wake nor sleep,
Like warriors roused before the zero hour
And shot, and frozen, standing in the light
Reflected from the snow, colder and colder,
Erect in horrible torpor, facing dark.

Love is a witless exile in the dark,
Delirious outcast, wretchedest of all,
Like a gaunt dog in a hallway, out of the cold,
Starving to death through numb and slower sleep,
Hurt only by experience of light,
Foolishly fed in dissolution's hour.

O in this hour, this agony, this dark,
Who knows what light or music, clear to all,
Waits beyond sleep, the other side of cold?

Rolfe Humphries

METROPOLIS

I dreamt that suddenly the metropolitan sky
Closed in its dark dome a million dead,
Blindly and soundlessly, merciless like lead,
Shut in a huge tomb that company
Of mad imperial men. I heard their cry

Fade as the door closed, and as the stone
Rolled on their lust and laughter I saw
One most beautifully spared like Noah
Reaching towards me. His blood and bone
Through a pellucid miraculous prism shone.

'I am Shakespeare,' he said, and then I knew
How Hamlet hung like a vision in his eye,
Questioning my right to live or die:
Lear and Othello in a storm of dew
Whose passion and tragedy we travel to.

'I too am Christ.' His lips were red
With the bitter vinegar he'd rinsed thereon.
O like a classical bird his heart bore on
My fate like an omen. 'I come,' he said,
'With Calvary's disaster on my head.'

Strange in a dream, alone with that man, I stood
At the world's centre, while east and west
Winds worried the nostril of each beast,
The sun shone, birds hopped, leaves of the wood
Lay embalmed in an unreal solitude.

'Shakespeare and Christ, the bright and brittle blade
That splinters with power the city sky,
This is the nerve you live and labour by.'
I remembered the huge tomb, its million dead.
'O what of those mad imperious men?' I said,

And woke. And suddenly the metropolitan sky
Broke in a thousand fragments. I heard
Shakespeare shouting his innumerable word
Louder and louder — the creed, curse, cry
Of men in history.

                                      John Hall

CRISIS

Now that the seas are lined
  Vith fire, and a fathom under
  Vaterspouts prepare,
In the salt cold, their thunder;

Now that the land is warm
  For the due rain, for the seed,
But war birds, dropping sulphur,
Drone, and the borders bleed;

Now that the ways are strangled,
Now that the best has been,
Where lies the hidden pathway
Verity walked in?

Still hidden; as when blue peace
Clouded no other sky,
And would not name our death dates,
Nor answer how and why;

Nor happen along these pavements,
Lightening with news
The feet wherewith we stumble
Still, cursing our shoes.

                    Mark Van Doren

INVOCATION

O Thou, Creator from original Chaos,
What shall we ruinous men

Offer Thee, war at end, for new creation
But chaos again, our cloudy aspiration,
Formless still as the smoke of burning cities?

Or plans, a tumult of plans, the architecture
Of Babel and dark dream —
   We, vowed to what inveterate delusion
   That leavens Truth, near whole, with vast confusion
Moving to laughter and tears the heavenly Pities?

Oh brood on our good-will, Thou only goodness!
Redeem our faith, our hope
   From vanity! Engrave upon our vision
   The human image of divine precision,
The lovely finite, clear in limb and feature:

And lay Thy hand, Thou only master-builder,
On human hands; oh build
   A polity, from the shaken world's commotion,
   Larger in wisdom, worthier devotion,
And man in man's free service Thy new creature!

                              G. Rostrevor Hamilton

DOMINE, DIRIGE NOS

Direct us, Lord, while our aerial saints,
Directed by their passion for this land,
Repel with zeal that slackens not, nor faints,
Each onset of the devastating band.

Direct, in this our broken sleep, our dream
Of Thy celestial city, which we share

With them who, in the four-year war, could deem
No loss too high, so they might scale her stair.

Still let our pity be a rustless sword,
Miraculously purged of sanguine stain,
Drawn forth but in obedience to Thy word,
And at Thy word thrust in its sheath again.

                                    E. H. W. Meyerstein

TWO WAR SONNETS

THOUGHTS OF A BRITON IN THE FOURTH YEAR OF WAR

How far away the nights when I could sleep,
When I gave up my mind to loving hands
Invisible, and seemed to lie on sands
Over which the waves of a wide sea would creep
With pearly monotone, serenely deep,
Murmuring tranquilly, 'He understands
Our music. See! his trusting heart expands;
Into his dream let no wild engine sweep!'

Now am I lullabied to wakefulness
By terrors of the air without, within
By thoughts that I have lost touch with the time.
There is no respite from this new distress,
Where solitude is measured as a sin,
And Peace, that gleamed a virtue, looms a crime.

THUS ANSWERED

Is it no comfort that a million share
Vigils of one, who thinks himself alone;
That empire of machines is overthrown

When single brains unsocial fancies dare;
That ever hearts which resolutely care
For their land's freedom stifle not their groan,
Knowing that, vented, even this may atone
For the grim burden of the hours they bear?

A multiple Prometheus is mankind,
Chained to the rock for its inventions vast,
Pecked by the vulture of material thought,
And so far-seeing that its sight is blind,
While the fierce warder mocks at the repast
Wherewith the nights, till succour come, are fraught.

E. H. W. Meyerstein

TAKE UP THE WINGS

Deliberately chime
The sounds that end a year.
Fallen, the bird of time
Is terrible and near,
And death seems everywhere.

The beak and claws are red,
Cruel the jewelled eye;
But see the vast wings spread
That, before the will must die,
Had crossed so wild a sky.

By these we, too, must rise
Or leave all flight undone,
Ignorant of new skies,
The farthest seas, the sun
Lighting the wide unknown.

Now fly with the strong wings
Of ended history.
Listen: The blind wind sings
The brightness we shall see,
The spirit rising free.

We move as a god once moved,
Beating a storm on the reeds,
Toward the form so greatly loved;
And body with vision speeds,
Bearing the future's seeds.

We dream of a new world,
As Icarus on his height —
Glad, should the sea wait curled,
To signal in our flight
The flooding source of light.

Lawrence Lee

THE FIRE-BRINGERS

Prometheus knew:
There was the chain
And the abominable bird.
But still fire grew;
And, warmed, men heard
The prophecy out of pain.

The moral wrong,
The body's shock,
All ways that hate may move —
However long,

Longer his love,
Less yielding than the rock.

Now strike the beaks,
All blood, again
In unclean legions free;
Each hour breaks
New Tyranny
Over the mind of man.

Know and endure:
The seed of flame
Springs up a field of light;
The fire you bore
Prepares in night
Bright mournings with new name.

Lawrence Lee

THE ATTITUDE OF YOUTH

We were told that wars are made by the makers of munition,
And therefore we must resist them, now as before;
Not knowing that wars can be equally made by the prophets of
      perdition;
Who rankle under defeat, till they make one war the more.

We were told that nothing was sacred, all things were ours for
      the taking.
That old age was hypocrisy, youth the one thing to find.
And from that dream of ours we have no desire to be waking,
Though it be but a dream, we will seek it, drunken and blind.

The thousands on thousands bombed, the millions fleeing in
    terror,
Are not of our flesh and our blood, however wretched their
    plight.
We are finer and better than they. This war was a ghastly
    error.
We must go on as we were, shaking our fists at the night.

Till the fields are all reaped, and the ditch is filled at another's
    bidding;
And death behind barbed wire awaits for the man who resists.
Till the hoarse voice from the depths blesses the bloody wed-
    ding;
And we sacrifice life in vain, for the one chance that we missed.
                           John Gould Fletcher

WE THAT ARE OLD

We that are old have little will
    To linger on;
Life may be well enough, but still
    The zest has gone.

Yet if death came for us one day
    We should feel cheated;
The hope, for which we crave to stay,
    Would be defeated.

We live each day, we live each night,
    With a dumb pride,
Confident we shall see the right
    Yet justified —

Shall see that monstrous braggart strength
      Crushed and down-borne —
Confident that the world at length
      Will share our scorn.

Yet, to drop out and miss the thrill
      Of exultation
That spreads and surges — as it will —
      Through all the nation —

To die, obscurely confident
      Not clear-assured,
That were indeed a banishment
      Hardly endured.

But should death swoop down from the sky
      With rush and roar,
An old man may be proud to die
      Who dies in war.

He stood where heretofore they stood
      Who were the strong,
·He fell as men fell who made good
      Their names in song.

Though not in limb or sinew staunch
      He kept reliance,
The soul unshaken still could launch
      Supreme defiance.

So, through swift dark or lingering light,
      Let our goal be
Death's honour — or, at last, delight
      In victory.
                      Stephen Gwynn

THE FESTIVAL

The 'cello sobs, the symphony begins,
The fever flutters in the violins,
A hundred earrings tremble in the dark,
Sleek in their velvet squat the seven sins:

And sauntering down the river you and I
Discern the baffling planets in the sky,
Through the tall branches watch the tell-tale feet
And hear the voices of the summer sigh.

The castle fades, the distant mountains fade,
The silence falters on the misty glade,
The ducal lantern hovers on the hill,
The cathedral moves into the evening shade.

Softly upon you falls the casual light.
Your hair grows golden and your eyes are bright
And through the warm and lucid Austrian air
In love our arms go wandering to-night.

Far to the east extend the ancient seas,
The dear Danubian banks, the archaic trees
Among whose pillars still the restless dead
Dispel their homesick odours on the breeze;

Crete blows the night across her wicked floors
And Sicily now locks her little doors,
And up the Adriatic leap the clouds
And hurl a shadow on her sucking shores,

And northward through the benches of the park
Stealthily moves the thin conspiring dark;
The thieves and fairies huddle by the bridge
And hear the sickly hounds of Brussels bark.

Each hungry orphan climbs into his bed
Afraid to face the usual midnight dread;
Across the cobbles past the pock-marked church
The hags go hustling with their crusts of bread,

The cripples stumble slowly up the stairs
And toss their curses on the stuffy airs,
The cellar-eyed, the sleepers in the ditches,
Mutter their simple paranoiac prayers.

Listen, the rhythms of the night begin:
The little lamps are flickering in the inn.
Out through the door into the garden glides
The fretful elegance of the mandolin.

The night flies on, the coming tempest flies,
And all our lovely neighbours close their eyes.
Silent the paths of longing and regret
Which all our learning taught us to despise,

And you and I look out upon the stream
And by the lantern's mild and mirrored gleam
The inverted figures on the shore perform
The silly baroque postures of a dream.

O who is there to answer you and me?
The sky, the summer, the prolific sea?
The ground is shaking and we must not wait
Who one more moment feel alone and free,

And hear the angels with their wingèd fears
Like serpents hiss their carols in our ears
And rediscover on this festive night
The hatreds of a hundred thousand years.

Frederic Prokosch

SANTOS: NEW MEXICO [1]

Return to the deep sources, nothing less
Will nourish the torn spirit, the bewildered heart,
The angry mind: and from the ultimate duress
Pierced with the breath of anguish, speak for love.

Return, return to the deep sources, nothing less
Will teach the stiff hands a new way to serve,
To carve into our lives the forms of tenderness
And still that ancient, necessary pain preserve.

Oh, we have moved too far from these, all we who look
Upon the wooden painted figure, stiff and quaint,
Reading it curiously like a legend in a book —
But it is man upon the cross. It is the living saint.

To those who breathed their faith into the wood
It was no image but the very living source,
The saviour of their own humanity by blood
That flows terribly like a river in its course.

They did not fear the harshness nor while gazing
Keep from this death their very precious life.
They looked until their hands and hearts were blazing
And the reality of pain pierced like a knife.

[1] Santos are small wooden figures of the saints, carved by journeyman artists for the village churches and altars in the eighteenth and nineteenth centuries.

We must go down into the dungeons of the heart
To the dark places where modern mind imprisons
All that is not defined and thought apart:
We must let out the terrible creative visions.

Return to the most human, nothing less
Will teach the angry spirit, the bewildered heart,
The torn mind to accept the whole of its duress
And, pierced with anguish, at last act for love.

                                        May Sarton

SOMETHING PRIVATE

Waking this morning to a glory
Of birds and slant light in the orchard,
A mad diffusion of honeysuckle
On the air, and fields dew-hoary;
I rubbed my eyes with a sleepy knuckle,
Stung them to watchfulness nurtured
On delight in the day, I put behind
The sirens of night, the terror
Of bombs, and children consumed with fire;
Deeds of pride and the evil mind,
Of mothers' sons warped in the mirror
Of a madman's doctrine and desire.

Though knowing my post in the burning city,
My duty to neighbours in the street,
The need for teamwork rather than pity,
All heroics subdued and discreet,
And discipline so necessary and dull;
Still along my nerves I heard the feet

Of dancing life, and in my brain the pull
Of daydawn ideas, things to be done
Intimately, creation in private
Joy, engendered by the sun,
Then cast for all mankind to have it.

                            Richard Church

A HOUSE IN WAR TIME

Look at this ancient house; it has survived
Three centuries of time, and human history.
Things have grown old in it. Grandfather clocks
Have frayed much catgut hauling down the hours;
Pot handles have worn smooth, and poker knobs
Been polished by palms long folded over breasts
Now quiet and untroubled in the churchyard.

Search any corner here, attic or cellar,
Odd pantry cupboard or a gunroom shelf;
You'll find the throw-outs of ten generations,
Household rubbish made romantic by time,
Print bonnets, bundles of letters, broken toys,
Pathetic vestiges of civilised life,
Emblems of peace and a continued growth
In one place, in one faith, of civil man
And all his works.

                    Here is the centre of it,
That long activity in hope; the plans,
The achievement, the discarded and replaced
All gathered in this house beneath a roof
Where the bats hang, and hermit spiders lurk.

I should be sure enough of all I hold
Within such walls. I should look out through windows
Set three feet back in mellowed brick and stone,
And stand secure amid my universe
Now turning to its rich, late summer days,
Life's discipline grown fruitful. I should see,
Like some old patriarch in a lost religion,
My wife and children round me, the fulfilment
Of mutual love beyond the need of words.

Instead, I hear the wind wail in the walls,
By night and day I hear the fleets of death
Pass overhead, to deal out mutilation
On those who have no quarrel with the sky,
But look to it as their forefathers looked,
For rain, for sunshine, for the busy song
Of larks in spring, and movement of the stars,
Those symbols of a God half-understood.

The ancient house dissolves. My lifework thins,
And a reverberation tears it down.
My gathered harvest is consumed in fire,
Thunder, and fire that flashes in their eyes,
My loved ones, gone down in their agony.

The raid is done. The sky is clear again
For stars by night, and singing lark by day.
Eternity once more puts on the mask
Of time, to hide its dreadful wisdom from me.

Still, after peril, stands my house foursquare,
Still, with the nightmare passed, I may contrive
To comfort those I yet may call my own.
The clock ticks on, the bat and spider keep

A sacred shadow in the roof above.
Laughter, love's fullest echo, fills the house.
Nothing has changed, except that Universe
I dared to raise, before I looked on fear.

Richard Church

THE HOSTING

We did not believe. This anger is surprise,
A cold flame out of an unexplored heart's core;
Suddenly we must search in each other's eyes,
Nothing remains as before.

So much a part of life our intimate dream
That air and water were its counterparts,
As unregarded and as good. And now the stream
Dries, the gasping starts.

While we could choose, we chose. That hour is gone by;
There is no longer time for weighing or fear.
Simply, we cannot breathe, and so must die
Out of our atmosphere.

Now we need neither drums nor high words to say.
The secret heart decides unalterably.
We draw together, quietly facing one way:
The rest are the enemy.

Brooke Byrne

EPITAPH

We were not many, and no bronze asserts
Our unheroic living between the ultimate guns.
We the despised, whom no allegiance supports.

Our spiritual country was a bridge.
It went out in the floods. Not even the piers remain,
No ford for crossing from hostile edge to edge.

Or we were divers under the wave of the world,
Living precariously out of our native air,
Clumsily swung in a world where blood is cold.

They had names for us, the not-quite-single-brained,
The dubious and unvaliant, the exiled, the finally dead:
Who neither fought nor surrendered, and died unclaimed.

There was no great need to kill us in haste.
The smoke of the burning books, the folds of the flag,
We stifled in them as others died in the past.

Having learned silence, we went to the earth
And practised silence, or spoke to silence forever.
Be merciful: it was our condition of breath.

Brooke Byrne

TO MY SON

Now the blackout of frontiers
Between home and gehenna
Kills the light in the eyes

That would speak to you, throttles
The word in the throat, estranges
Us from ourselves. Our soiled pledges
Have become a bundle of lies for the ragpicker's sorting
When the bombers are still, and the bottles broken.

How shall we talk
To you who must learn the language
Spelled on the fields in famine, in blood on the sidewalk?
Child (can I say?)
When the night roars, remember
The songs we sang, lapped in the warmth and bright
Of the nursery:
Malbrough s'en va t'en guerre
Ne sait quand reviendra.
Farewell and good-bye to you, Spanish ladies,
Farewell and good-bye to you, ladies of Spain.
Memory stifles thought.
The lamp makes a stain on the floor.
Youth is the time to dance. No more:
We have lost your music.
The iron that rings the brain,
The leaden weight in the hollow
Breast where the heart should beat,
Remain.

I cannot hide you now,
Or shelter you ever,
Or give you a guide through hell.
You are ignorant, you are unarmed, and behind your
Scornful smile I see you are deeply afraid.
History threatens you at each street-corner,
The seas are sewed up, and the colors fade
On every map you studied early and well.

The driven exile discovers
Midway in an obscure wood
What does not bloom for the fool:
The flower whose root is despair.
You, in an obscure room in a masterless school,
Must find the faith that cements
The promises public events and private blunders left broken.

Are you alone?
This I would tell you, this I would have you remember,
Who felt your heartbeat, boy, before you had breath to cry with.
This is the tragic matrix of all joy.
You must wrestle alone
In the naked night, like the Jew
Compelling the unkind angel.
If you fight in the dark
With your self till you force a confronting,
You will be blessed in the morning.

You will be blessed recalling
The question you asked as a child:
How can I change myself
When I have nothing to change
Myself with?   Then I smiled,
And told you: your will.
Now I know it is love
Of the impossible
That shapes the dove and the lion,
ᵁI tell you it is love
Of the impossible
That brings the soul to its own.

Though I can hardly reach you and never prove
What the event will teach you,

I, who am helpless to move
You from the road you choose,
Or alter the face you will meet there,
Leave you these words with my love.

Babette Deutsch

HISTORY

Once it was packed like a box with the toys of childhood,
Even the largest dolls grown small and familiar,
And the cuckoo clock saying,
'Tomorrow, tomorrow.'
Once it was sad and comic like Mr. Punch,
And events jumped up, like Judy, to be whacked
Over the head, and the greatest kings, like actors,
Were happily at once alive and dead.
Once it was apart
As a crumbled castle on a darkening slope
Half-seen from the express.
But whether it was tall as towers or
Tumbled with playthings like the nursery floor,
It was remote and faithful.

History,
Coming too close,
Is monstrous, like a doll
That is alive and bigger than the child
Who tries to hold it.
It is a clock that cries the thirteenth hour.
It is a theatre
On fire.
History now

Is not the empty castle but the train
Emerging from the tunnel, running
Down the embankment toward the modest station,
Where it will lie like a box of toys, broken,
Unpacked in vain.

                                                    Babette Deutsch

TO A YOUNG FRIEND

You asked me:
Cannot youth save the world?
Cannot the young build here, on this earth, a shining house,
Out of our hearts, out of our good intentions?
And I made some stupid reply;
I think I said, No.
Now that you are gone, I think, as always, of the things I should
        have said to you:
How youth is a seed, falling across the earth,
Blowing over the land, forever blowing, forever falling;
How some of it finds good soil, and grows with beauty,
How some of it withers to death among the stones . . .
Here, in one spot, roses; and elsewhere, the desert.
(Someone else said that, long ago; — do you remember?)
Loam and sand, the seed falls, it cannot keep from falling.
How youth is a wave, rolling away in all directions,
Part of it to break against rocks, or die on the beaches,
Or in the great calms —
And yet, how the wave itself must rush on, foaming, far out into
        the distance,
Into the darkness . . .
And the next wave,
And the next,

Forever rising, forever breaking . . .
Those are the things I should have told you.
I do not know why I did not remember them.

Robert Nathan

THE STOICS

They were the oaks and beeches of our species.
Their roots struck down through acid loam
To weathered granite and took hold
Of flint and silica, or found their home
With red pyrites — fools mistake for gold.
Their tunics, stoles and togas were like watersheds,
Splitting the storm, sloughing the rain.
Under such cloaks the morrow could not enter —
Their *gravitas* had seized a geologic centre
    And triumphed over sub-cutaneous pain.

Aurelius! What direction did you take
To find your hermitage?
We have tried but failed to make
That cool unflawed retreat
Where the pulses slow their beat
To an aspen-yellow age.
To-day we cannot discipline
The ferments ratting underneath our skin.
Where is the formula to win
Composure from defeat?
And what specific can unmesh
The tangle of civilian flesh
From the traction of the panzers?
And when our children cry aloud

At screaming comets in the skies, what serves
The head that's bloody but unbowed?
What are the Stoic answers
To those who flag us at the danger curves
Along the quivering labyrinth of nerves?

E. J. Pratt

LEGACY

Wars end, and men come back from them
Into another world not of their knowing,
And strangers they to their own blood and bone
Who remember them before their going.

Dumb with what knowledge, blinded by what light:
Of strange ways and dreams, and alien-speaking;
Sit they thus and stare beyond the hills
Or, lost, walk restlessly forever seeking

That time they knew, the place, the word;
As children tricked by a conjurer's illusion,
Children with puzzled eyes, and oddly old,
Confused at their own sad confusion.

Frederick Ebright

IN THE FOURTH YEAR

September 3, 1939–42

Over this huge escarpment, valiant heart,
  This triple ridge deep-girdled by dark cloud,
This league of struggle sternly set apart,

Strive on and up, to steadfast service vowed!
You that have seen the crown within the cross
  And courage radiant in the bombed abode,
You that can rise on wings above your loss
  And never count defeat but as a goad,
What weeds are gathered where resolve is strong?
  What fears grow rankly, glorious land, in you?
Dim is the dawn delayed, the night is long,
    But through the cloud the mountain gains the blue.
      Strive onward, to the hidden sunlight rise,
      Toil as your friend and Freedom as your prize!
                    Gorell

IN TIME OF SUSPENSE

Draw-to the curtains then, and let it rain.
We'll look no more on that disordered scene:
Blind rage upon a blinded window-pane,
The shivering white upon the darkening green;
Nor that beyond it, leaping to and fro,
Ghost in the ruined garden, or mad briar?
Shut out confusion, draw the curtains to,
Build the cathedrals of the fire anew.
Close, eyes, on doubt, and open on desire.

Here, in the quiet brilliance of belief,
We fashion life at such intensity,
The very chairs might rustle into leaf
And panels grope to build their primal tree.
Now when our bodies meet like star and star,
Now when our minds remoter commerce do,
No wish too subtle and no world too far,

But we, so perfectly in tune we are,
Passionately conceive and make it true.

And so farewell to Winter, for I hear
The lambs rejoicing on a hill of jade,
The blackbird in his vocal graph of fear
Scattering darkness down the painted glade.
It crowds the curtains, mad in bud and wing,
That world of passion that your fancy craves,
That England that the fancy, quickening,
Cannot but call the very eye of Spring,
Lashed by the curled abandon of her waves!

Folly of dreaming, when you have entwined
Wild arms about the dreamer and the dream!
Drawn by those gentle Avons I shall find
A land where April does not merely seem.
Narrow horizons! Yet how wide to me
For whom they compass all those island charms
That I must die to safeguard, it may be:
An England the aspiring candles see,
Narrow enough to compass in my arms.

So in this room. But when I stood alone
One evening on a windy crown of land,
Beneath the emblem of a youthful moon,
And watched oblivion like a tired hand
Folding the map of Spring away, I knew
Hill upon hill receding were no more
Than picture and faint effigy of you,
Nor shall I ever after lose that view
Though I descend into the night of war.

For us, no heartening slogan will assuage
What must be suffered in the mad descent.
We dreamed that war was but an awkward age
And country could be lost in continent.
The cretin world remains where it began,
Clings to the shambles and improvement shelves.
Too undeceived for patriotic man
Youth takes up arms to rescue what it can;
For all is lost, but what we have ourselves.

When war came to our cradles once, it meant
Only the mutter of a thunder-clap
Somewhere beyond the tidy hills of Kent,
A black line every morning on a map,
Germans in the allotment, trains unlit —
Did we not learn of war in gentle doses?
We merely breathed it like a dangerous grit
In every breath we drew, contracted it
From our warm bottles like tuberculosis.

Formed by the years of agony, wherein
Fear stole into the heart and set up house,
Formed to be nervous as a violin,
We find no brothers in the dead. For us
No voice will speak in the white cemeteries
Of France. We are not of that careless kind
To whom life seemed to offer prize on prize,
Who, at the terminus, with laughing eyes
Saw only joy in battle. Blind, stark blind.

Nor are we of the next unhappy age
That laughed, with laughter hollow as an urn
Raised to belief, the murdered heritage.

Now from those ageing pantaloons we learn
The young are very serious. Even so.
As passionately serious as the Spring
After the sterile gaieties of snow.
Give us but time enough, and we will show
These barren valleys how to laugh and sing!

Give us but time, we say. For now, on all,
The radiant anguish of a dream is thrown.
Vivid the bird beyond the orchard wall
Who fills Goodnight with poignancy unknown.
More beautiful because it is more haunted
Our world revolves. Accusing as a text,
These walls, these shapes of love we have been granted,
Are critically watching though enchanted:
'This Winter, yes,' they nod at us. 'But next?'

Thus for the island genius, Liberty,
Much loved by Roman letters in our stone,
Another generation learns to die
Gravely, not caring if the flags are flown,
Believing simply it must save for Earth
A way of life becoming to mankind,
A grace of centuries, a thing of worth:
This we believe, who by a peaceful hearth
Have laughing eyes to-night, but are not blind.

Then let the violin on its own nerves
Be racked, if only the sweet Master seek
The harmony its brittle heart conserves.
What if, while you and I contrive to speak
With exiled April in a distant room,
The clouds should lift, and a young moon outside

Swim like an amulet beyond the gloom?
Shall we not look upon this night to come?
Blow out the candles — throw the curtains wide!

Laurence Whistler

IN THE TIME OF THE PERSECUTION

Down in the river the fishes are rising,
Golden or green in the sun or the water.
Up in the sky the birds and leaves chatter.
I lean on the bridge in a twilight-disguising
Of anguish at heart and bitter surmising.

The willows and aspens in shuddering whispers
Speak for my sorrow: the rooks in their flying
Pack in their darkness the weight of my crying.
The spread Western reds are my Good Friday vespers.
Only the word of a Malachi prospers.

I have become a scourged limb of my nation,
Limb knowing limb where Israel lies bleeding.
My flesh feels the whips that mock its wild pleading.
The Adam within me forgets the creation.
I cover my head in the old lamentation.

Forgive me, my England, forgive me, sweet river,
Forgive, church and inn, forgive, foster-mother;
But to-night I must turn to the maimed, homeless brother,
To Warsaw, Lublin, nay! to all Europe over,
Even to France that once was my lover.

And you who have taught me the meaning of people,
You, oh my Christ! Who taught me the lonely
And marvellous mission of seeking You only
To find all my fellows, forgive! From Your steeple
The bells shall give tongue when the new tyrants topple.

But now by the river, when night drops its fringes,
And muttering sounds are the prayers of the dying,
I turn from lament to the stern, ancient crying:
'Lord God of Hosts! The God of revenges,
Pour down Your plagues on the wild beast that ranges!'

Hunt it that mauls us, as once the cruel Pharaoh.
Drive it to earth, and let the last killing
Be eye for an eye, Your justice fulfilling.
Spare not its cubs; beware of their sorrow,
For the sake of our morrow, of Europe's to-morrow.

L. Aaronson

PERSONAL VALOUR

If once we feared that Fear itself might come,
A lodger with a ·retinue of slaves,
(Despair, misgiving, doubt, and other knaves),
To make within our soul their shameful home,
Like some dishonourable malady
Concealed from all but our own private knowing,
Our own concern that there should be no showing
Of·fear of Fear, that worst worm enemy,

— Now that our danger rises like the sun
Chasing all thin confusing mists away,
How fine, how proud, our wings of courage sweep

Clear as a sea-gull for each separate one,
Poising ourselves above our island spray
Around the bastions of our lonely keep.

V. Sackville-West

NOVEMBER 11TH, 1942

Sun in the mist this morning,
And still, damp, cold,
Like half-forgotten, half-remembered old
Mornings; the new dawning
Of the old day.
Am I to say
That in the morning fog
I saw the final cog
Engaged, and the machine turning?
In the mist could I see sprockets striving,
And tracks spraying the sand,
To culminate three dreary years of learning
So late, of what we wouldn't understand,
And the completed mechanism driving?
The turret guns in the big hangar,
Traversed aimlessly with empty shell-racks
Through sweet exhaust smoke and efficient clangour,
Seemed to lay pathetic aim,
Impotent, upon the same
Target in the desert tracks.
This is the end of the beginning;
The end of making
And the start of breaking
The enemy's impregnable construction
Where it is waned and thinning,

Of building up our ruins by destruction.
Moon in the mist this afternoon,
And looking up from learning to forget
I seemed to understand that soon ·
I might be able to remember
How a misty sun would set,
Shadow-shrouded like a midnight ember,
With a wet blush on russet bracken,
And all the insubstantial world would slacken
Under the dim surveyance of the moon.
With the end of the beginning
Comes the beginning of the end,
When we who kill and shatter just to mend
Are winning;
And all the separate vital pieces
Of the whole immense machine
With convulsing tracks are seen
In sudden action racing
Towards the ultimate crisis
 Vhere victory builds the basis
Of complete destruction, and releases
Us from all the future ruins we are facing.
Mist in the dark to-night,
And though I cannot see the lake,
There oily ripples break
The muffling fog with dimly radiating light,
Indicating beauties of to-morrow,
Which mist, like sorrow,
Now blankets out of sight.

                              Lawrence Toynbee

ON GOING TO THE WARS

I do not go, my dear, to storm
The praise of men; this uniform
May shine less gay in gas and mud
And be medallioned but by blood,
While lips that know your lips will turn
Uneasily to harlot worm.
And war, it's true, fouls both the flesh
Victorious and the flesh it slays.

   Yet must we play the beast afresh
To claw from wolves their power to craze
The heirs of Raphael and the kin
Of Bach, our friends the foe.
I, too, let's say, a travail owe:
So that our son, who curls within
The womb, may wake to brighter earth,
I must not shrink from giving birth
To death.   I go that he may stare
Blue-eyed into Canadian air
Unhaunted by the charnel birds
That drop their excrement of death.
I go that he may draw free breath
To speak the rich and ancient words
We use, and spell from books unburned,
And teachers not from trueness turned.
I march that he may learn from grass
And rose what we have missed, the pass
To quiet life, and never set
The rendezvous my father met
In vain.

I go that we may breast
Again the Dorset downs in zest
And walk the Kentish lanes where I
Began a larger life in knowing
You. Yet if from seething sky
I win reprieve but by the slowing
Crutch, or whitened cane, my doom
Will yet have helped to hold in bloom
Old English orchards and Canadian
Woods unscarred by steel, Acadian
And Columbian roofs unswept
By flame. My mother will be kept
From stumbling down a prairie road
Illumed by burning barns and snowed
By patterned death.
                    Is it so rash
To seek to rank with men who saved
Your English father from a lash
In London streets, and bent head shaved
Because his mother was a Jew
Who starved last year in Lodz? And you —
My dear, I'll not survive to see
You bricked within a ghetto slum
In Canada, by booted scum.
I pledge that if by chance I flee
The blundering malice of the guns
I'll stand by those who strive to chart
A world where peace is everyone's,
A peace that does not rot the heart
With hunger, fear, and hopeless hate,
Nor rust the cunning wheels nor still
The subtle fingers, peace that will
Unlock to every man the gate
To all the leaping joys his hand
Creates. For no less prize I stand.

And now, my dear, since we may yet
Delight in leaf uncrinkling, and
In maple woods the violet,
Then let us from the patient land
Take strength, nor fail to share the charmed
Routine of stars, or trysting keep
With common things, with evenings warmed
By music, food, and love, and sleep.

For present solace these, but for
Our hope we've nowhere else to look
Except into our spirit's book.
No hell unspilled by lords of war
Upon the people's flesh has ever
Parched the human heart's endeavour,
The human will to love and truth.
For one face mired in black unruth
A score will signal us each day
The sun unquenched within our clay.

Across the tundra of our dread
We must beat on, windbitten, to
The unseen cabin's light, and through
The glooming western firwoods thread,
In hope to pass the peaks terrific,
And win the wide sundrenched Pacific.

Earle Birney

COWARDICE

In journeyings my weak soul makes
And breaks the pestilence of swarming sin,
I am the traveller through the burning lakes
That bears the body with the message in.

I am the field of war, where Good and Bad
Mingle and batter and break, striving for place
Like well-matched warriors making an Iliad
Behind the fixed-flesh barrier of my face.

Though battles and adventures over-again
Possess this celluloid within my skull
Bones must escape the circumstantial rain,
Blood must remain unspilt, flesh plentiful.
The play must stay in print, avoiding action
Or else the text will suffer in translation.

Emyr Humphreys

COURAGE

Who of the eternal future will read
Of the dead when they were prepossessed with death
Will judge by what they did not what they said
The hour the minute the moment the last breath.

Prepare now the cause for a decent action
Manipulate the plot towards the crime
The personal crisis in the national situation
The prison the wall the bandage and the lime.

Swing the emotion to the heroic pitch
Then whip the fleshy horse over the deadly ditch.

Emyr Humphreys

THERE IS NO SANCTUARY FOR BRAVE MEN [1]

There is no sanctuary for brave men,
   Danger allures them as it were a sun;
What they have dared they will dare once again
   And so continue till the day is done.

There is no satiation of brave deeds,
   One draws another as wit calls on wit.
Oh, what a soul it is that ever heeds
   The hour's necessity and springs to it!

There's no intimidation of great thought,
   Knowledge attracts it as the heavens the eye;
Though dangerous 'tis to learn, it will be taught,
   Pushing its question to the uttermost Why.

There is no sanctuary for brave men,
   Danger allures them as the moon the tide;
What they have dared they will dare once again
   Though they lose all else in the world beside.

A. G. Herbertson

DESCEND, O DANTE

Descend, O Dante, from the Heavenly Rose,
   Light our lost way with your star-dusty feet.
   We are beset with those devouring foes
You fled, those bestial ancients that repeat
   The old familiar tactic of the Beast,
   Marking the quarry, cutting off retreat.

[1] Reproduced by permission of the Proprietors of *Punch*.

Nor leopard, lion, wolf, has ever ceased,
    Though you avoided them, to stalk the prey.
    Now, woe! we are that prey, we are that feast.
The allegory shifts and symbols stray,
    The dramatis personae change their roles,
    But menace looms as dark as yesterday.
Worldly delights take daintily their tolls;
    Imperial pride, and property for power,
    Those primal greeds, haunt still our hungry souls.
We are devoured of sin, and we devour.
Return, O citizen of Heaven, to Earth's blind hour!

O pilgrim spirit, turn your purgèd eyes
    Again to time, from your eternity;
    From light unveiled, to shadow and surmise.
Look down upon our storm, O eyes that see
    The scattered leaves of all the universe
    Ingathered in Love's Book of Prophecy
Fulfilled. Look down, great exile, and rehearse
    With us the steepness of the alien stair;
    Taste yet again, with us, the salty curse
Of beggars' bread. Come from your Otherwhere
    Of vision, to us perishing. Descend,
    And share again the old distraught despair
Of exiled peoples trapped in hate's dead end;
    Of conquered nations, bogged in hope's decay;
    The desert-dreams of prisoners who pretend
To freedom. Hark, the homing souls astray,
Crying for light! Come, Holy Candle, light our way!

                                        · *Florence Converse*

DIDO OF TUNISIA [1]

I had heard of these things before — of chariots rumbling
  Through desolate streets, of the battle cries and the danger,
And the flames rising up, and the walls of the houses crumbling,
  It was told to me by a stranger.

But it was for love of the fair and long-robed Helen,
  The stranger said (his name still troubles my sleep),
That they came to the windy town he used to dwell in,
  Over the wine-dark deep.

In the hollow ships they came, though the cost was dear.
  And the towers toppled, the heroes were slain without pity.
But whose white arms have beckoned these armies here
  To trample my wasted city?

Ah, this, Aeneas, you did not tell me of:
That men might struggle and fall, and not for love.

                Phyllis McGinley

'THEY ALSO SERVE...'

Imagination flies out on the airman's wings,
  Country by country, city by city, it maps below;
I've lain in sand all day dreaming of shade and springs,
  Slept on anemones under Olympus' snow,
Heard in my ears the undying song that Freedom sings,
  As over ridge and river of Greece we stayed the foe.

But oftener in the winter nights I've waked and tossed
  On heaving Atlantic, where my restless soul would be,

[1] Copyright, 1943, by *The New Yorker*.

When the moon was man's enemy and the Arctic frost
   Glittered upon my halyards; or from Sicily
Watched the sun's glare for treachery, while to Crete I crossed,
   Treading in foam the vintage of the Ionian Sea.

But there's an agony bitterer than the unfettered mind
   Can mirror — hideous in the darkness and blood-reek
Torture of captives, groaning as the mills that grind
   Beauty and health to horror and to dust the weak.
Oh to be free to die for comrades, for mankind!
   These cannot die nor live, who durst not hear nor speak.

I could not bide disfranchised from the bodily fray,
   Tending my flowers in peace beneath a friendly sun,
Were not my spirit at war adventuring night and day.
   The spirit of Man besieged, the world's ends overrun,
Truth keeps her citadel; here my soul shall stand at bay
   Steadfast, a private sworn in Freedom's garrison.

I could not bide, and watch the loveliness unfold
   Of English earth, for which the flower of youth must die —
Life at their hazard bought, secure, inglorious, old —
   Had I not faith that Beauty bids me to defy
Death in her name, that Truth has trusted me to hold
   Humbly, in turn, at her good hour, her torch on high.

Oliffe Richmond

AFTER HEARING THE PRIME MINISTER, APRIL 27TH, 1941

My God, I thank Thee that my course is set,
with others of Thy choosing, at this hour;

to see the right discerned, the challenge met,
and battle given to the evil power;
to share the upward thrusting to the light
and all the grandeur of the stony ways;
to know the heart's contentment in the fight,
O God, with our election in these days.
Too great inheritance and too much ease
cheat mortal vision of immortal things:
then welcome, these redeeming agonies,
these ardours and assaults, this fiery faith
and all the purifying blaze it brings,
this part of Champion and this march with Death!

Richard Elwes

WAR

Cold are the stones
That built the wall of Troy,
Cold are the bones
Of the dead Greek boy

Who for some vague thought
Of honour fell,
Nor why he fought
Could clearly tell.

Innocence, hired to kill,
Lies pitilessly dead.
Stone and bone lie still.
Helen turns in bed.

Patric Dickinson

WORLD WITHOUT END

A world is breaking. Midnight's bell rings down
The fable-founded stones of palace walls;
The swallows and the merchants both are flown;
The rooftree of the temple rocks and falls.

Yet peopled is the fallen mart and court,
The altar served whatever ill be done;
The forms of man's unalterable thought
Carve still their timeless perfect Parthenon.

Age cools the fevered stars: they fall, they die.
Stone crumbles, iron rusts, to thankful rest:
Man's Spirit rooted in divinity
Springs on inviolate within the breast

Of Time, and grows not old nor hard nor cold
Whatever cloaks of flesh impede and mar,
Building anew each towering-tumbling world
From dust, from fallen star.

                                        Patric Dickinson

NOT REVENGE...BUT THESE

Is my wrath splendid? Yet I become
a heart of sorrow, lips made for pain,
eyes that see only to give tears;
anger without endurance swears to avenge
my numberless deaths; when the dead are with me
earth has no blossoming, the stars no light,

but above all, the sacrificial innocents
no consolation. . . .

I say, I will be God, my terrible arm will strike
fire from stone, flood from the gentle stream,
embattled, I would march before Israel; Yet I become
the mother, infinitely suffering, endlessly sad;
the agony is itself, what has it to do with revenge?

Only the recompense of resurrection is just,
the whole made whole, scars erased
from bewildered eyes and the innocents restored;
O God, only these. . . .

Not the waiting
in the night for memory to cease; far lands
beckoning escape from the afflicted earth;
not the penalty unto the third and fourth generation
upon these children; not grief in immortal measure
for the defeated; O God, not these. . . .

Only the gracious heart returned,
the summer-blossoming soul and the kindled stars;
children unafraid in meadows, laughter
billowing from the unsinister skies;
God, only these. . . .

Emmanuel Litvinoff

THE PHOENIX

The Phoenix said to me
(That wild and lovely bird in the ash tree
Which never in its double-score of springs

Bloomed with such dark wood-opal glimmerings
As dropped from the purple fall of his shut wings) —

Calmly, incuriously
The Phoenix said to me,
'After so many a year do I return:
As always, I behold the trampled seed
And I behold again the roofs that burn
And I behold again the men that bleed.

'Is it so forever?' Quietly while I gazed
He stooped his head to the gold fruit I raised:
'Again, and again, and again
Shall the shouting massed armies pack the plain,
Slaying and being slain?
Poor men, you toss away your warm live breath
As if there were no death:
Believe me, goodly though you stand and brave,
Strong jaws has the grave.'

I answered with a proud and passionate word,
'O brightest creature ever seen or heard,
O loveliest bird, still you are but a bird!
Born and re-born albeit eternally,
You see not understanding what you see.
It is because death *is*, and sets a bound
To our life's little round —
It is because we have a flesh too frail
To long outwear the gale —
It is because our thought and our desire
Burn us away like fire —
We dare cut narrower yet our narrow span,
And to die steadfastly
In a good cause for conscience' sake, shall be
And is, the glory and the crown of man.'

Very clear and bold
That sardonic topaz eye
Ringed with transparent gold!
He rose, and standing high
Settled those plumes that on the dazzled sight
Glowed like a tropic night.

He said, 'Blue as a gentian is your sky;
The small fields lie
Russet and olive and emerald-hued between
Hedges of quicker green.
— So much for any gathering hand to take!
Do you do wisely for whatever sake
To cast away a world as rich in bliss,
Beauty and mirth, as this?'

I answered, 'We do well to lightly hold
Even this fair earth, which being prized too high
Would fail us sorely in our growing old.
Though it delight the eye,
If we should feed our hearts upon it, slowly
We should dwindle, spirit, flesh and bone —
For man, that cannot live by bread alone,
Lives not by beauty wholly.'

Preening the prismy feathers of his breast,
Replied the bird — 'I never had a nest,
Nor ever had a son,
Nor shall have one:
But see, the star-flowered strawberry plants run wild
Along the ditch, and look, a two-years' child
Chuckles and fills his hands with coral fruit.
— Tell true or else be mute!
Do they do well, whatever good they seek,

Who change the dimpled cheek,
The close arms, the warm breath
Of child or love, for the embrace of death?'

At first I had no voice —
Remembering one who made that bitterest choice
And made it smiling.   Afterward I said:
'O Phoenix, these our dead
Knew as we know that all the best in life —
Lover and child and wife,
Being once possessed cannot be lost to death:
This is our faith —
That they are part of us as we of them —
Flowers of one stem.

'But if it were not so —
Too well we know
That even man's tenderest tie of love is less
Than that divine duress
Which rather than suffer him to live in shame
Drives him upon the steel, the flame.

'We are as you, O Phoenix! dying in fire
To rise with glory from our little dust:
We trust, we are bold to trust
That in itself the existence of desire
Argues desire's fulfilment — that to climb
Presumes the crest achieved in God's good time —
And that to dare to die, for such as we
Is evidence enough of immortality!'

                              Audrey Alexandra Brown

THE WARDEN'S WATCH: 2 A.M.

The night is still; the quarter moon slips down
Through ever deeper orange toward the west.
A plane drones out to seaward on some quest;
The shifts are changed; the warden guards the phone.

Such nights see famous cities overthrown,
Seething with flames like a volcano's crest,
Norwich and Bristol, Coventry, Plymouth, Brest,
Kiel and Rostock, Bremen and Cologne.

The night is still; but many a pillowed head
Turns half-attuned for that unhallowed wail
Which bodes the aerial firedrake flying near.

Deep in the dumb unconscious lurks the dread
Of man's own monster spewing deadly hail;
Yet stand and wait means but to sit and hear.

Robert W. Cumberland

DAWN

O Holy Light! Thou who art strength!
The morning yet is far, sullen with doom.
This is the hour of fear, the night of storm.
Man's ancient refuges are wrecked,
His mercies fled.
The ways of peace are hidden from his eyes.
Grant now the vision that he sense
Thy glorious dawn beyond the battle-smoke.

Mankind, aye, thy mankind
Is sorely sieged by hate's black hordes
Armoured by cruelty,
And sworded by bleak Death.
Bitter the night that now assaults his will,
Yet holds he fast.
Calmly, remembering thy holiness,
He fronts his foe unwavering.
Though weary from the desperate fight;
Lit by the flickering guns, he stands
A rock of safety to his friends,
While hate's mad legions rave about his feet.

O Holy One, thine own mankind is he!
I who have glimpsed the coming dawn,
And seen the victory
Shining beyond the battle-fog,
Would call to him the vision thou hast given.
O be thou proud of him! his will
So like thine own. Open his spirit-sight,
Grant him swift flashes of the coming joy.
Thine are the gates of triumph and of day
That ope with shout of jubilance and song!

O Holy One, here in the battle ruck
Ere comes thy light, stand thou by him,
Place on his shoulder thy strong hand,
And when the new day breaks across the world
The foe shall see his banners crush their hate
With triumph, and the splendid dawn shall shew
The star-gemmed crown of victory on his brow,
The God-lit heavens thundering hymns of joy.

                          Ernest Fewster

PANIC

We are ill of a new wind
streaming through our barricades,
ringing on the sword grass blades,
harsh with peril,
clapping in the empty canyons.
Alarms and danger
tolling on that wind,
rolling thunders and sudden cannonades.

We are ill of a strange moon
spinning in our lakes and streams,
from hissing waters and sea-screams
too soon risen,
coming too fast across our mountains.
Fires and danger
flaring in the moon
that glares upon us in our angry dreams.
                    Rosamond Dargan Thomson

THE TROPHY

The wise king crowned with blessings on his throne,
The rebel raising his flag in the market-place,
Haunt me like figures on an ancient stone
The ponderous light of history beats upon,
Or the enigma of a single face
Handed unguessed, unread from father to son,
As if it dreamt within itself alone.

Regent and rebel clash in horror and blood
Here on the blindfold battlefield.   But there,
Motionless in the grove of evil and good
They grow together and their roots are twined
In deep confederacy far from the air,
Sharing the secret trophy each with other;
And king and rebel are like brother and brother,
Or father and son, co-princes of one mind,
Irreconcilables, their treaty signed.

Edwin Muir

*

XXII. WOMEN AND THE WAR

*

MOTHER OF GOD

Mother of God, all tenderness and truth,
All reverence and beauty, and the seal
Of heavenly love, pray for the sins of men!
Without your intercession at the throne
Where sit the Almighty Father and Your Son
Our wars, ambitions, devilries, crimes and greeds
Bulk to the depth of doom. We have our strengths,
Those attributes of greatness, that outride
The forces of the night, but they have been
On many a hearth and over many a field
Age-long oppressors of the mild and meek.
Man's dominance has been a fortress held
With dour tenacity against the plea
For equal justice and life's enterprise
Borne upon level scales: we need so much,
Such places in the sun, such power, such words
Of praise and comforting, but, most of all,
We need forgiveness — never man was made
Who, unashamed with every thought revealed,
Could stand before the judgement-seat and claim
To be assayed as an uplifted soul
Beside the purity, the quiet peace,
The ceaseless drudgery and uncomplaint,
The sacrifices and the selfless dreams
That may abide within a woman's life.
We take our stand: we labour and we strive,
Strive for our honour and the hope of fame,
Our dignity, our passage through the world,
Devote ourselves to service and to death,
But always on us falls the centred beam
And we are paid our price. For Womanhood

Throughout the ages of the earth has stretched
The unapplauded, devious mountain-track;
Even now, when slowly broadening into life,
Often all silent is her starry way.
Pray for our sins! The prayers of women rise
Out of the carnage of this man-made strife,
Above the horrors of the slaughtered world,
These empty conquests and ensanguined fields:
In every church, by every wayside shrine
The kneelers ask for mercy, Mother of God,
Not for themselves but for the lives they tend.
The patient mothers of the human race
Lift up those voices little heard on earth
Into the kinder heaven, the sisters, wives,
And all to whom Life's lily is in flower
Ripened by Youth and Hope — how deeply they pray!
Lean out of Heaven, hear them, pardon all
For their appealing, all the cruelties,
The evils, errors, and the saddening gulfs
Of good intent. Their tears are manifold:
Their hearts unspoken, like a flock of doves,
Beat with white wings about the throne of God.

Gorell

WIDOW-MOTHER

Soldier boy, soldier boy,
  Gallantly you go —
Head erect and shoulders squared,
  Marching heel and toe.

The tale repeats itself, my dear.
  I stood thus, smiling so,

> To watch your father marching — five
> And twenty years ago.
>
> And I am proud again. Again
> A tear comes full and slow.
> Can a heart be broken twice?
> Presently I'll know.
>
> *Ada Jackson*

LA FEMME DE QUARANTE ANS

I was born forty years ago.
I lived . . .
a little girl with blowing hair.
I grew . . .
like a flower
in that garden of security.
I knew no fear
in a world of five-per-cent security
How superficially beautiful it was!
I married.
I was happy.
There was war.
He went for king and country.
He died for them.
He died with the other millions.
He left me with a son.
That was all that was left of him.
The boy grew up.
There was war.
He went for king and country.
He went in the air.

Like an eagle he went.
They shot him down.
And he died.
You have seen things fall
from a great height.
That is how he died.
Do you know who I am?
I am the woman of forty.
I am English.
I am French . . . German . . .
I am Russian . . .
I am the woman of forty.
My men are dead.

Stuart Cloete

THREE THOUSAND YEARS AFTER [1]

That time great Hector stayed and comforted,
Before Troy's wall, white-armed Andromache,
His infant feared the helmet on his head,
Which he laid down, and then laughed merrily.
Today our soldier lags his brave goodbye
At narrow tenant door or cottage gate,
His child grasps at his boat-shaped hat, held high,
And laughs his baby powers to celebrate.
What though no lofty wall of storied fame
Towers here as on that day of ancient woes!
This wife is strong as was the Trojan dame,
The brimming joy of childhood overflows:
And Hector's laugh that stilled his infant's fears
Is deathless song to bridge three thousand years.

Edith M. Tuttle

[1] Reprinted by permission of the author and *The New York Times*.

*

XXIII. PEACE

*

PHOENIX

Rise from thyself, thou phoenix world,
O wings consumed, arise;
From those inflaming anarchies
Torrentially hurled

Around thee by thy lone self-will,
False despotisms, ires,
Suspicions, inadulterate fires,
Finalities of ill,

Arise, and be thyself, the bird
Of frankincense and balm
Nursed on the elemental palm,
Whereof our hearts have heard,

O myth, O angel of the East!
Sink not in western flame;
Renew thy nest, re-win thy fame,
Purged, cindered, and increased!
E. H. W. Meyerstein

ONE MORNING THE WORLD WOKE UP

One morning the world woke up and there was no news;
No gun was shelling the great ear drum of the air,
No Christian flesh spurted beneath the subtle screws,
No moaning came from the many agony-faced Jews,
Only the trees in a gauze of wind trembled and were fair.

No trucks climbed into the groove of an endless road,
No tanks were swaying drunken with death at the hilltop,
No bombs were planting their bushes of blood and mud,
And the aimless tides of unfortunates no longer flowed:
A break in the action at last . . . all had come to a stop.

Those trees danced, in their delicate selves half furled,
And a new time on the glittering atmosphere was seen;
The lightning stuttering on the closed eyelid of the world
Was gone, and an age of horizons had dawned, soft, pearled,
The world woke up to a scene like spring's first green.

Birds chirped in waterfalls of little sounds for hours,
Rainbows, in miniature nuggets, were stored in the dews,
The sky was one vast moonstone of the tenderest blues,
And the meadows lay carpeted in three heights of flowers:
One morning the world woke up and there was no news.

Oscar Williams

RETREAT [1]

When there is peace again, soldier, what will you do?
    I shall go back to the job I had before
    Behind the counter at the hardware store —
        That's what I'll do.

And you, sailor, when you have left the sea?
    I shall go back to my job as a plumber's mate,
    And lean of an evening on my garden gate —
        That'll suit me.

[1] Reproduced by permission of the Proprietors of *Punch*.

What will you do, brave man with the silver wings?
  I shall return, I hope, to my pre-war life,
  To my dog and my week-end golf and my wife
    And such-like things.

And I myself, what is my heart's desire?
  I want to go back to a house that is all mine,
  To lie in one of my own chairs on my spine
    By the fire.

Back, back, is where all of us want to go,
  Each to his little well-worn well-loved spot;
  So who in the wide world's going forward is what
    I'd like to know.
                Virginia Graham

AFTERWARDS

When the grey night is pierced
By the rose-lipped rays of dawn,
And the night of nations' agonies
Makes way for ecstatic morn:

When the shell-drowned songs of summer
Thrill once again the sun-bound air;
I shall return to the hills of heaven
And hear the songs of silence there.
              Peter Baker

NOTES ON CONTRIBUTORS

*

AARONSON, L. He lives in London, England.

ALLAN, MABEL E. An English writer, living in Cheshire.

ALLFREY, PHYLLIS. Mrs. Allfrey lives in London and is an adviser in an Air-Raid Relief Station. She has published *In Circles*, a book of verse.

AUSLANDER, JOSEPH. Lecturer on Poetry, Columbia University; author of several volumes of verse; Chief of the Poetry Division, Library of Congress.

AYLEN, ELISE. She lives in Ottawa, Canada, and is the wife of Dr. Duncan Campbell Scott. She has published poems and plays.

BACON, LEONARD. He has written many books, and won the Pulitzer Prize for Poetry in 1941.

BAKER, PETER. A younger English poet, author of *The Beggar's Lute*.

BENÉT, WILLIAM ROSE. Mr. Benét is Associate Editor of *The Saturday Review of Literature*. He has produced many books, including both poetry and fiction.

BERRYMAN, JOHN. An American poet; instructor in English at Harvard.

BINYON, LAURENCE. A distinguished English poet; for some years Keeper of Prints and Drawings at the British Museum. He served as C. E. Norton Professor of Poetry at Harvard during the session 1933–34, and lectured at the University of Athens on English poets for five months during 1940. His translations of Dante's *Inferno* and *Purgatorio* are well known. He died in March, 1943.

BIRNEY, EARLE. Dr. Birney is Associate Professor of English in the University of Toronto. He recently published *David and Other Poems*. He is serving with the Canadian Army.

BLUNDEN, EDMUND. Mr. Blunden has been Fellow and Tutor in English Literature at Merton College, Oxford, since 1931. He was on active service during the First World War and has published *Undertones of War* (prose). He has written many poems, which have been collected from time to time in book form. Since September, 1940, he has been one of the officer-instructors with the Oxford University Senior Training Corps.

BOGUSLAWSKI, ANTONI. Colonel Boguslawski is a popular Polish poet, with a distinguished military record. He has produced five volumes and several translations. Major Lewis E. Gielgud, of Polish descent, has translated *Dawn*, the poem included in this collection.

BOURINOT, ARTHUR S. A Canadian poet, living in Ottawa. He has published several volumes of verse.

BRADBURY, BIANCA. Miss Bradbury lives in New Milford, Connecticut.

BROWN, AUDREY ALEXANDRA. She is the author of two volumes of verse, *A Dryad in Nanaimo* and *The Tree of Resurrection*, and lives in Victoria, British Columbia.

BROWN, HARRY. He is a Staff Sergeant on active service abroad with the American Engineers.

BROWN, HILTON. An English poet.

BROWN, IVOR. A well-known English poet, novelist, and dramatic critic.

BURLINGAME, ROGER. Writer of verse, articles, and short stories. During the First World War he served on the Western Front with the A.E.F.

BYRNE, BROOKE. Miss Byrne is a Second Lieutenant in the Massachusetts Women's Defense Corps, the women's branch of the Massachusetts State Guard.

CHURCH, RICHARD. An English poet, novelist, and critic, living in Kent.

CLOETE, STUART. He was born in Paris, was educated in England, served with the Coldstream Guards, and farmed for many years in South Africa. He is both novelist and poet. His latest volume (verse) is *The Young Men and the Old*.

COFFIN, ROBERT P. TRISTRAM. He won the Pulitzer Prize for Poetry in 1936. His latest volume is called *There will Be Bread and Love*.

COLMAN, MARY ELIZABETH. A Canadian writer, who lives in Vancouver, British Columbia.

CONVERSE, FLORENCE. Miss Converse is both a poet and a novelist. She lives in Wellesley, Massachusetts.

CUMBERLAND, ROBERT W. He is Assistant Professor of English in the Cooper Union for the Advancement of Science and Art, and is a Precinct Training Commander in connection with the Air Warden Service.

DANE, CLEMENCE. Distinguished English writer of plays, poems, fiction, and essays.

DAVIES, DUDLEY G. He was a member of the Indian Civil Service till 1928, and is now connected with the Home Guard, after having been head warden of the Local A.R.P. from 1939 to 1941. He is a rector in the Church of England.

DEUTSCH, BABETTE. American novelist, poet, and critic.

DICKINSON, PATRIC. He was invalided from the British Army after a severe accident and is now connected with the B.B.C.

DUNSANY, LORD. He has written many plays, poems, and stories, and was on active service in the First World War as a

Lieutenant in the First Battalion, Coldstream Guards, and as a Captain in the First Battalion, Royal Inniskilling Fusiliers.

EBRIGHT, FREDERICK. He is a Technical Sergeant in the Finance Department of the United States Army.

ELWES, RICHARD. Lieutenant-Colonel Elwes saw service in France as Staff Captain to an infantry brigade and returned to England through Dunkirk. He is co-author with his mother of *Gervase Elwes*, a biography of his father.

FEWSTER, ERNEST. Dr. Fewster lives in Vancouver, British Columbia.

FLETCHER, JOHN GOULD. An American poet, living in Arkansas. He was awarded the Pulitzer Prize for Poetry in 1939.

FROST, FRANCES. An American writer, living in Spring Valley, New York.

FROST, ROBERT. A distinguished American poet. He has received the Pulitzer Prize for Poetry four times, and also the Gold Medal of the National Academy of Arts and Letters. His latest book of poems is called *A Witness Tree*.

GIBSON, WILFRID. A prominent English poet, with more than twenty volumes to his credit. He was a private in the Army Service Corps during the First World War.

GORELL, LORD. A well-known English poet, who during the present war is serving as a Company Commander of the Home Guard in part of Sussex. He was Captain and Adjutant of the Seventh Battalion, the Rifle Brigade, 1916, and became a Major on the General Staff, 1918.

GRAHAM, VIRGINIA. An English writer.

GWYNN, STEPHEN. An English poet and essayist, living in Berkshire. He saw service in France during the First World War as Captain, Connaught Rangers, with the Sixteenth Irish Division.

HALL, AMANDA BENJAMIN (MRS. J. A. BROWNELL). She is engaged in Red Cross activities and work for the Navy Relief in the United States.

HALL, JOHN. A younger English poet.

HAMILTON, GEORGE ROSTREVOR. He is a permanent civil servant in England and also a well-known poet and essayist, having published several volumes of prose and verse.

HARRISON, ELIZABETH. Mrs. Harrison is painter and poet. She lives on Garden Island, near Kingston, Ontario.

HERBERTSON, A. G. Miss Herbertson is an English writer.

HILL, AGNES ASTON. A Canadian poet (of Calgary, Alberta), whose sonnet 'Recompense' won first place in a recent competition.

HUDSON, DENIS. He is serving in the Royal Navy as an ordinary seaman.

HUMPHREYS, EMYR. A Welsh writer.

HUMPHRIES, ROLFE. An American poet. During the First World War he was a First Lieutenant in the machine-gun branch of the infantry. He was awarded a Guggenheim Fellowship in 1938.

JACKSON, ADA. An English poet, author of *World in Labour*.

JEFFERS, ROBINSON. An American poet living in Carmel, California. His latest volume of verse is entitled *Be Angry at the Sun*. His *Selected Poetry* appeared in 1938.

LEE, LAWRENCE. He teaches French at the University of Virginia and is the author of *The Tomb of Thomas Jefferson*.

LEITCH, MARY SINTON. Mrs. Leitch has published several volumes of verse and has edited an anthology, *Lyric Virginia To-day*. She has also written plays. Her home is in Lynnhaven, Virginia.

LITVINOFF, EMMANUEL. An English poet, author of *Conscripts*.

LUCAS, F. L. Fellow and Lecturer of King's College, Cambridge, and University Lecturer in English. He is an able critic and poet, who has published a number of books, including *Tragedy, Studies French and English*, and *Ten Victorian Poets*. He saw service during the First World War in the Seventh Royal West Kent Regiment and Intelligence Corps.

'LUCIO.' He is a frequent contributor to *The Manchester Guardian*.

MAGEE, JOHN GILLESPIE, JR. Pilot Officer John Gillespie Magee, Jr., was born in Shanghai, the son of the Reverend and Mrs. John G. Magee, of Washington, D.C., who spent many years as missionaries in China. After preparatory work at Rugby, he came to the United States in 1939 and gave up a scholarship at Yale in order to enlist in the Royal Canadian Air Force in September, 1940. He served overseas with an R.C.A.F. Spitfire Squadron and was killed in action on December 11, 1941, at the age of nineteen. He wrote the sonnet 'High Flight' after a flight into the stratosphere.

MALCOLM, GEORGE. Major George Malcolm, the younger, of Poltalloch, Scotland, is on active service in the Middle East.

MARTINEAU, G. D. A British officer and poet.

MASEFIELD, JOHN. He succeeded the late Robert Bridges as Poet Laureate of England in 1930. His work as poet, playwright, and novelist is widely known.

MEYERSTEIN, E. H. W. An English poet who has published also plays and fiction and has written a biography of Thomas Chatterton.

MICKLEM, NATHANIEL. Principal of Mansfield College, Oxford, and the author of several books, one of the latest of which is entitled *Theology and Politics*.

MIDDLETON, J. E. A Canadian poet and literary editor of *Saturday Night*, Toronto.

MILLAY, EDNA ST. VINCENT. A well-known poet and playwright, who has published several volumes. She won the Pulitzer Prize in 1922.

MILLS, CLARK. Instructor in French at Cornell University and author of a volume of poems entitled *A Suite for France*.

MINSTER, LEO. An English writer on literary and historical subjects.

MUIR, EDWIN. A Scottish writer living in St. Andrews.

McGINLEY, PHYLLIS. An American contributor to periodical literature.

MacLEISH, ARCHIBALD. A distinguished American poet with fifteen volumes of verse to his credit, for one of which, *Conquistador*, he received the Pulitzer Prize in 1932. He has been Librarian of Congress since 1939.

NATHAN, ROBERT. Mr. Nathan's work in poetry and criticism has won him a wide audience.

NEWTON, MURIEL. An English writer who for the last two years has been an organizer for the W.V.S. She lives in Dorset.

O'CONOR, NORREYS JEPHSON. Author of a number of books and at present Chairman of the Language Section of the Local Defense Council in Pasadena, California.

O'HEARN, WALTER. He is a Sub-Lieutenant in the R.C.N.V.R.

PATTERSON, FRANCES TAYLOR. An American poet.

PEAKE, MERVYN. He has published *Shapes and Sounds*, a volume of poems. He has served as both gunner and sapper in the British Army.

PERRIN, JOHN. Dr. Perrin worked in a hospital in the East

End of London during the first two years of the present war, and is now a member of the Royal Air Force Volunteer Reserve.

PRATT, E. J. Professor of English at Victoria College, the University of Toronto, and author of several volumes of poetry.

PROKOSCH, FREDERIC. He has produced five novels and three books of verse, including *Death at Sea*, which contains many of his latest poems.

RICHMOND, OLIFFE L. Professor of Humanity in Edinburgh University. During the First World War he served as a Captain in the Intelligence Corps at the War Office and at Italian Headquarters. He has published classical studies and also two volumes of verse, entitled *Rawalpindi* and *Song of Freedom*.

ROBERTS, CHARLES G. D. Sir Charles, an influential Canadian writer of long standing, lives in Toronto.

ROWSE, A. L. Mr. Rowse, of All Souls' College, Oxford, has published *Poems of a Decade, 1931–41* and will shortly publish *Poems Chiefly Cornish* and *The Spirit of English History*. He has written many studies in history and politics.

SACKVILLE-WEST, V. The novels, studies, and poems of the Honourable V. Sackville-West are widely known. She is the wife of Mr. Harold Nicolson and lives in Kent, England.

'SAGITTARIUS.' An English poet who contributes to *The New Statesman and Nation*. She is the author of a volume of verse called *Sagittarius Rhyming*.

SANDBURG, CARL. A widely known American poet, author of a biography of Abraham Lincoln, for which he received the Pulitzer Prize in 1939.

SARTON, MAY. Miss Sarton has contributed many poems to American periodicals and has published a collection of her verse called *Inner Landscape*.

SCHIFF, CHARLES. He practises medicine in England.

SCOTT, DUNCAN CAMPBELL. A Canadian poet of long standing, whose home is in Ottawa.

SMYTHE, DANIEL. He is a Sergeant in the United States Army and has published a volume of verse entitled *Steep Acres*.

SPALDING, HELEN. An English writer, working in the Ministry of Economic Warfare.

SPENDER, STEPHEN. He is a well-known English poet and essayist, who is now connected with the National Fire Service as regional organizer of discussion groups.

STEVENS, WALLACE. Mr. Stevens is a lawyer and a poet. His books include *Harmonium, Ideas of Order, The Man with the Blue Guitar*, and *Parts of a World.*

STRINGER, ARTHUR. Long identified with Canadian life, Mr. Stringer, poet and novelist, has for some time lived at Mountain Lakes, New Jersey. He has published thirteen volumes of verse.

STRUTHER, JAN. Mrs. Joyce Maxtone Graham uses this *nom-de-plume*. She lives in Sussex and is the author of *Mrs. Miniver* and of many poems, articles, and short stories.

THOMSON, ROSAMOND DARGAN. She is the wife of Mr. S. Harrison Thomson, Professor of History at the University of Colorado.

TOYNBEE, LAWRENCE. He is the son of Professor Arnold Toynbee, and is serving in the British Army.

TUTTLE, EDITH. She lives in Paterson, New Jersey.

VAN DOREN, MARK. An American poet and critic whose latest volume is entitled *Our Lady Peace and Other War Poems*. He is serving as an air-warden in New York City and as a member of various writers' war committees.

VANSITTART, LORD. Lord Vansittart was Under-Secretary of State for Foreign Affairs (1930–38) and Diplomatic Adviser to the Foreign Secretary (1938–41). He has published several volumes of verse.

WELLS, ELEANOR. A young writer, who graduated from Wheaton College, Massachusetts, in 1940.

WHISTLER, LAURENCE. A well-known English poet, author of *In Time of Suspense*.

WHITE, T. H. He is a graduate of Queen's College, Cambridge, and writes both poetry and fiction. Two of his recent novels are *The Sword in the Stone* and *The Ill-Made Knight*.

WILLIAMS, OSCAR. An American poet, author of *The Man Coming Toward You*, and editor of anthologies entitled *New Poems, 1940*, and *New Poems, 1942*. A third volume in the series will appear in 1943.

YOUNG, ANDREW. He is an English poet living at Tunbridge Wells.

*

INDEXES

*

Index of First Lines

Index of Titles

(The titles of sections are set in small capitals)

Index of Authors